Postmodernism

Postmodernism

The Twilight of the Real

Neville Wakefield

PLUTO  PRESS

London · Winchester, Mass

First published 1990 by Pluto Press
345 Archway Road, London N6 5AA
and 8 Winchester Place, Winchester
MA 01890, USA

British Library Cataloguing in Publication Data
Wakefield, Neville
  Postmodernism: the twilight of the real.
  1. Culture. Postmodernism
  I. Title
  306

  ISBN 0–7453–0341–2 hb

Library of Congress Cataloging-in-Publication Data
Wakefield, Neville, 1963–
  Postmodernism: the twilight of the real.

  1. Postmodernism.   2. Civilization, Modern–20th
century. I. Title.
B831.2.W35   1990   306'.09'048   89-26623
ISBN 0–7453–0341–2 hb
ISBN 0–7453–0471–0 pb

Typeset in Plantin and Omega by BP Integraphics, Bath
Printed in Great Britain by Billing and Sons Ltd, Worcester

Contents

1 Heresies

One of the most harmful habits in contemporary thought is the analysis of the present as being, precisely, in history, a present of rupture, or of high point, or of completion or a returning dawn. The solemnity with which everyone engaged in philosophical discourse reflects on his own time strikes me as a flaw. I think we should have the modesty to say to ourselves that, on the one hand, the time we live in is *not* the unique or fundamental or irruptive point in history where everything is completed and begun again. We must also have the modesty to say, on the other hand, that even without this solemnity – the time we live in is very interesting.

Michel Foucault, interviewed in *Telos*

We might, in paraphrasing the science fiction writer Philip K. Dick, see introducing a book on postmodernism as something like trying to build a universe that doesn't fall apart. An impossible task – a mad project since we live in an era stripped of transcendent truths, linear arguments, solid foundations and neat resolutions. The ground upon which we tread is much more shaky. Structures tend not to last, grand theories tend to fade, ambitions have half-lives. Postmodernism is neither an homogeneous entity nor a consciously directed movement. It is something much more ill-behaved, nebulous, elusive, de-centred and de-centring. The universe that we build into the narrative of books (even books which take as their object the splintered, fractured world of postmodernism and postmodern theory) tends to suggest a coherence that is absent from the world which they may describe. Small projects take on grander overtones as we attempt to map this shifting ground. The writing subject may suddenly find him or herself imbricated in the very structures that they sought to dismantle, the 'grand' ambitions to which they had never aspired. The plot can suddenly thicken. And we can then find ourselves held hostage by the very thing that we believed we could explicate and control. The universe once again becomes unsteady as we find that we have built structures (whether born of rationalist positivism *or* apocalyptic fatalism), that are too rigid, too coherent and too explicatory to survive in a world of flux. And we are reminded, as we must be reminded continually, to return to something more modest ...

All writing is in one way or another autobiographical – this book being no exception. It is therefore without apologies that this introductory section concerns my own encounter with what has come to be termed postmodernism, its genesis and subsequent trajectory. It is a sketchy and fictional chronology which is ushered in with the publication of a text by Jean Baudrillard entitled *Simulations*, which first appeared in translation in 1983. For me this was, and quite possibly still is, the single most provocative text to enter the postmodern debate. In attacking the umbilical relationship between the sign and the 'real' world that it supposedly refers to, Baudrillard threw into crisis the premise of all semiotic or structural analysis – the project of escorting the reader from an exterior world composed of legible signs to an interior world of order and understanding. The text itself no longer had the reassurance of the formulated critique, but vertiginously collided forms of allegory, science-fiction and simulation. It constituted a triumphant sort of cynicism that was, on my part at least, greeted and even celebrated as the first truly postmodern (non)analytical text that delivered the anarchic world of signs from the asphixiation of outmoded discourses and their attendant methodologies.

The magnetic fascination exercised by Baudrillard's work proved to be more than a 'merely' adulterous diversion from the more sober body of critical (postmodern) texts that I was by this time attempting to make sense of, in the form of a thesis from which this present book is drawn. In this fascination/seduction I was not alone, a fact that was witnessed by a ballooning body of cloned 'Baudrillardian' texts as well as his own elevation to the status of cult figure. This was also beginning to affect the increasingly frustrating terms under which I was attempting to write the thesis, since it (specifically *Simulations*) refused to be assimilated within the corpus of 'critique' that I was studying, or to adopt a 'position' or set of positions within the debate that was supposedly being 'overviewed'. The tone of the work and indeed its justification rapidly began to shift from being one of evaluation and exegesis to one of cathexis. Increasingly Baudrillard appeared as the cuckoo in the nest, threatening not only to deprive the other habitants of sustenance but in the process to destroy the nest itself. Metaphors of exorcism and cathexis became ever more pertinent to the survival of the work as the guru role that was both self-appointed and adopted – as the 'evil demon of the image', 'the ideological Jacques Cousteau of the New York intelligentsia', 'prophet of the apocalypse' etc. – increasingly cast him as a sort of Kurtz to be confronted at the end of the river of withering signifiers.

All of this may well appear melodramatic, spuriously cooked up in order to help me through the tedious monotony of thesis writing, were it not that what seemed to be at stake here was the very future of criticism itself, and more parochially the future of the thesis that I was writing and its claims to have any relevance to contemporary, 'living' culture.

However, this dramatic rhetoric does, I hope, help to highlight the turbulences of a relationship which was later to be formative in the structuring of this book. The intellectual climate that provided the backdrop to my initial reception and assessment of Baudrillard's work was one that was steeped in the sort of structuralist analysis that seemed to grasp meaning only at the moment of ossification – in other words, an analysis that stultified its object by forcing it to prostrate itself across rigid and inflexible explicatory grids, an analysis which, to paraphrase Barthes, in 'capturing' life was actually 'seeing dead'. The problem was that in asserting the life of the object (over the subject) Baudrillard was also implying the futility of all criticism: the moment at which critical discourse loses its ability to distance itself from its object is the moment at which the performed critical *act* turns into the weightless critical *gesture* – in other words, its own simulacrum. This might well seem to provide adequate grounds for the termination of a relationship destined to plunge into depths of fatalistic nihilism. But the blind reaction that was the course taken by many of my contemporaries simply fell back onto the sort of analysis that I was sure was inadequate – it just refused to acknowledge change. Instead it clung onto old analytical structures and tired oppositional rhetoric, nostalgically recreating a Paradise Lost of an era that was, to use someone else's nomenclature, pre(Post)erous.

By this point it seemed clear that the 'crisis' announced in the convergent critiques of Enlightenment rationality, transcendental subjectivity and positivist science were utterly imbricated in the project that I was undertaking. The lengthy and difficult 'texts' which surround the postmodern debate and constituted the core of the study that I was undertaking, could not, after reading Baudrillard, simply be 'explained away'. As the implications of his work began to sink in, it became clear that the security of exegesis and evaluation was under threat. In rejecting the structuralist understanding of meaning I found myself working in an area in which deconstruction and the reflexive play of language substituted themselves for the evaluation and exegesis that, as a good Anglo-Saxon, I had been taught to cherish. It was a rejection that also, and just as alarmingly, saw the principles of dialectical reason replaced by those of seduction. None the less it remained the case that the crisis of postmodernism could not be related, let alone examined, without according Jean Baudrillard a central role on the postmodern screen (in the absence of a stage) and nor could the structuralist method adequately account for the way that meaning is generated and consumed in the early 1990s, even though accepting the full implications of these two provisos then defeated the possibility of writing a 'good' thesis. It was therefore a bittersweet irony that the thesis that was to become the basis of this book should have been praised as an exegetical and evaluative text. It is an irony that I would wish to be maintained in the reading of this account of postmodernism – as in a uniquely postmodern way there is the sense that where this book appears at its clearest and most successful in its elucidation of the terrain of postmodernism it is in fact at its weakest and closest to collapse. In a truly postmodern world the dividing line between the thing and its opposite is never stable; it is a world where clarity and obscurity, failure and success constantly exchange.

Alongside this autobiographical narrative is another alternative beginning which also charts a declension of faith. It is a story rarely told without a fringe of nostalgia born of a certain sort of moralism, since it documents a process of progressive disillusionment regarding the transformative powers of the artist, writer or critic and ultimately the withdrawal of those activities from the sphere of the political. Regardless of whether it is seen in terms of a metamorphosed relationship to politics, subjectivity, ideology, history, or any one of a number of other areas that have traditionally underwritten our authenticity as determining cultural beings, there is by now a consensus that this is a transformation that takes place under the sign of the 'post'. It is therefore ironic that in accumulating the cultural capital from which such a consensus can be drawn – a London bookshop lists over 6 pages of 'postmodern' titles – the 'post' itself has become exactly the sort of self-regulating system that it set out to analyse, gaining the appearance of autonomy, but losing any distinct sense of what has been lost or of what has been passed through. By looking specifically at Jean Baudrillard and tracing the trajectory of mutations that culminate in his denial of the political or any sense of the 'real' that could underpin it, I hope to restore some degree of context to a body of work that so often is taken to be free-floating and discontinuous.

The specific task of the 'Left' or the 'New Left' since the early 1960s has been to revise or expand traditional Marxist terms and categories to contend with what appeared to be a fundamentally new and crisis-free form of capitalism. The chief failing of the orthodox Marxist model of an economy divided between a stable productive base and an unstable mutable super-structure, continually subject to transmogrification within the flux of consumption, is that it does not describe the post-advertising world in which consciousness is not simply 'realised' but actually *produced* in the act of consumption. This, in highly abbreviated form, was the context from which Baudrillard attempted to salvage Marx's critique of capitalism from an outmoded attachment to a nineteenth-century vocabulary of production, class and a romanticised proletariate, when he published *The System of Objects* in 1968.

It is a collection of essays that focuses on consumption rather than production, and in its analysis of objects as signs not physical products provides the basis of a semiological neo-Marxism. A corresponding attempt to fuse Marxism and semiology distinguished many of the activities of the 'Situationists' who had reformulated capitalist society as a 'Society of the Spectacle' in which consciousness is produced, as our material needs are met, through a web of ideologically coercive 'spectacles'. According to the Situationist formulation of society, we no longer have access to a direct experience of reality since it is already mediated by capitalist ideology. That ideology, however, is itself 'real' and therefore offers itself as a site of intervention and resistance. Although alienation was still regarded as the inescapable social by-product of the capitalist system, it was no longer contained within the specific limits of exploitation and social inequity described by Marx, since according to the Situationists, alienation had by the early 1970s become infinitely more pervasive. It had penetrated the very process of signification. As early as 1968 Henri Lefebvre, to whom both Baudrillard and the Situationists were indebted, described a 'modern' world (*Everyday Life in the Modern World*) in which, 'alienation is spreading and becoming so powerful that it obliterates all consciousness of alienation'.[1]

Baudrillard's attempt to renovate Marx did not last long. The events that took place in May 1968, and the climate of disillusionment that followed, were perhaps formative in the break with Marx, a break which was formally announced in 1973 with the publication of *The Mirror of Production*. What was being criticised were the universal pretensions of Marxism's obsessive economism: the projection of the production goal over all previous periods and the phantasm of labour as the human essence. Because consumption, following its reformulation in *The System of Objects* had been shown to entail the commodity not just as an object but also as a sign through which the system itself is consumed – or more precisely, through which the system consumes its subjects – Baudrillard questioned Marxism's ability to articulate a critique of modern capitalism at all. What was announced instead was a deep complicity, in which Marxism was disclosed as the hidden mirror of capitalist political economy, sharing its belief in the primacy of work (labour) and the myth of human self-creation through production. If, as Marx claimed, the object is no more than the specular reflection of the subject, then production perpetuates the (capitalist) code through a steady stream of objects, each of which operates as another affirmation of the constitutive sovereignty of the subject. The paradox that emerges – one with which we are painfully familiar from the sustaining rhetoric of the Thatcher regime in Britain – is that for the capitalist system to continue unobstructed the subject must privilege the idea of his/her own autonomy. Production is therefore exposed as being the teleological substratum of all other values. It no longer exists primarily to meet and satiate needs, but to sustain the code.

The implications of this sustained critique of Marxism were not available to an English reading audience until the publication of the most well known and notorious of Baudrillard's texts, *Simulations*. Everything about this seminal text spoke of a radical break with what had gone before. Whereas the work prior to *Simulations* was attached (if negatively) to the established discourses associated with Marxism, sociology and social anthropology, the new text refused categorisation by hyperbolising these codes and spinning off into an entirely decentred postmodern non-space, in which fragments of science-fiction, Borgesian allegory, TV commentary, Disney politics and pulp ethnology intermingle and collide in a sort of Brownian motion that in its continual deferrals, deflections and collisions never allows the reader to indulge in the security of viewing the whole. Even the book itself, published in New York by Semiotext(e), refused to sit easily within the catalogue of knowledge that we so scrupulously shelve under disciplines, titles, authors, etc. It was small, slight and black – the sort of book that feels as though it might be illicit or illegitimate, designed to be glanced at during secretive moments on the move – and refused to take a place on the shelf for fear of being swamped or lost forever. In this sense it was reminiscent of the anarchic Situationist 'book' which was bound in course sand-paper so that once it was classified and delegated to the shelf it could continue to function anarchically and refuse assimilation by abrading the adjacent books. The Semiotext(e) series did not quite aspire to such an heroic ambition, but it did none the less refuse to be categorised within 'encyclopedic' systems of knowledge, and its anarchism, though of the softly softly cerebral sort, was no less provocative and abrasive.

It is ironically appropriate that a description of the cover of *Simulations*, its outer skin or dissembling surface, should correspond to, and even perhaps suffice as an explanation of its 'contents'. Although later on (see Chapter 9) we examine the genesis of the term 'simulacrum' via the 'three orders of the simulacra', it is enough for the moment to say that Baudrillard uses the concept of simulation as a corrosive means of attacking the assumption that signs can still refer effectively to a 'real' outside world that exists independently of them. In the simulated mediascape Baudrillard describes, the complexity of the intertextual flotation within media networks always confuses the story with the real event to the point at which images, codes, subject (the masses) and events (TV) flow and intersect independently of the referent. What is described is a hyperspace of neutralisation and indifferentiation, where dialectics has been given over to seduction, which brings with it a wholly new and violent rhetoric of demolition, inversion and provocation. In an era of simulation there is no reality beyond appearance and therefore no dialectics of inside and outside from which to position a critique. So not only is Marxism trashed and rendered untenable but so too is psychoanalysis, structuralism, cultural archaeology and all hermeneutics – in other words all systems of meaning/understanding that propose some 'real' latent content behind manifest appearances.

This is the advent of postmodernity, in which we have, to paraphrase Baudrillard, come out of history (and with it Marxism and theories of political agency and practice upon which the whole project of the Left rested) in order to enter simulation. The rest is, as it were, (post)history and belongs to the final chapter of the book.

In order to make sense of this highly schematic account of the 'history' of Baudrillard's ahistory it is necessary to return to 1968 and look at the changing role of the intellectual and how this might be mapped on to a move from modernity to postmodernity.

The tendency to blame academics and intellectuals for coining the term 'postmodernism' as part of their distinction games is the subject of an article by Zygmunt Bauman, 'Is There a Postmodern Sociology?'[2] In it he makes the claim that postmodernism in fact articulates the experience of intellectuals who face a status and identity crisis as a result of the decline in demand for their services – their legitimations no longer appearing important, as the grand narratives are replaced by fragmentary 'language-games' circulated by a new type of para-intellectual or cultural intermediary. Gone is what Dick Hebdige terms the intellectual as 'seer', 'the intellectual as informed but dispassionate observer/custodian of a "field of enquiry" armed with "penetrating insights" and "authoritative overviews", enemy of sophistry, artifice and superficial detail'.[3] Nor in a postmodern society can the intellectual fufil his or her traditional role as the 'bearer of universal values' since what Foucault termed the 'regime' or 'general politics' of truth has, if not disappeared entirely, certainly changed to the point at which it is barely recognisable for what it was. The status of those who are charged with saying what counts as true must change as the traditional means of discerning and sanctioning the truth are rendered incapable of situating the truth within the more general 'economy' in which the truth and the intellectuals circulate. It is a status which has changed both in fact and appearance – and we might well as a result tend to agree with Hebdige when he points out that, 'the putative signs of a "postmodern condition" sometimes look too much like the morbid projections of a group of marginalised, liberally educated critics trapped in declining institutions – the academy, the gallery, the "world" of art criticism – for them to be taken seriously at face value.'[4]

Following this line of observation, Baudrillard's relentless persecution of the real might appear to be nothing more than a desperate attempt to reinvest in the role of the intellectual after the manifest failure of their excursion into the domain or at least the political arena of the 'real' in 1968. The (postmodern) intellectual could thus disown his/her own impotence via the progressive destabilisation of the real and of the threat that it represented to an autonomy that was already on the wane. These are exactly the operational principles so tellingly described in the analysis of Francis Ford Coppola's film *Apocalypse Now*[5] – the reversability of destruction and production and the immanence of the object in its very revolution. For Baudrillard, the film *Apocalypse Now* in its 'excessive means' and 'monstrous candour' has become the prolongation of the Vietnam War by other means – the global cultural victory that offsets actual defeat at the hands of the Vietcong. Coppola's excessive deployment of cinematic power elevates the film into the historical world event, for which the war itself becomes no more than a pre-text. It is an analysis of the mechanisms of power that can also be found mirrored in Baudrillard's own project – in his relationship to the events of 1968, and his current veneration as cult messiah of the new world. The loss of the 'real', its progressive mutation into the critically disembodied state of hyperreality which has become the persistent leitmotif of every Baudrillardian text, now seems more than ever like the Copolla film, the completion of an incomplete war. The events of May 1968 are finally being granted the achievement that was immanent in their failure, and finding their apotheosis in Baudrillard's own work.

Twenty years on and the significance of this shift in the status of the intellectual is being metabolised under the all-encompassing sign of the 'post'. Baudrillard, who from the early 1970s onwards provided the most provocative articulation of this crisis, has now entered a period of review. His commitment to disband and ultimately to relinquish the traditional coordinates of practice and analysis that had positioned the intellectual firmly within a pre-established cultural topos has led to an indigestion for a 'theory' that fails to accommodate the most vital and sustaining part in the agenda of cultural criticism – namely the possibility of change. In retracting this component he has also retracted the justification for the discipline, its notions of academic or cultural endeavour, in other words its self-importance. What was initiated as a liberating critique of representation – for feminists a critique of patriarchal language and representational subjugation, for marginalised social and ethnic groups a critique of the univocalism and representational monotheism that denies them a voice, for the 'masses' a critique of a social theory of representation that promises to speak on their behalf – in Baudrillard's later work became an abnegation of the very possibility of representation. Epitomising an ambiguity that permeates all postmodern discourse, the Baudrillardian text liberates its subject only to see it die. Initially celebrated as a means of delivering history and the subject from the asphyxiating clutch of the referent, it is an account of postmodernism that now stimulates only a sort of intellectual diaspora as we witness the curious struggles taking place as 'reformed' Baudrillardians attempt a rapid disinheritance of their own 'bateau ivre' of postmodern nihilism. Baudrillard himself has become the heretic, once worshipped, now chastised for the lapse into 'asemism', a celebration of meaninglessness and a despairing assessment of the uselessness of all political action.

Within this climate of disavowal and wholesale dismissal, Baudrillard's account of postmodernity might seem to be of declining relevance to contemporary cultural theory. However, as the term 'postmodernism' and the name 'Jean Baudrillard' continue to attract a wider public interest it must be in part due to their capacity to speak of some of the changes that our culture is currently undergoing. The disillusionment with which his later work has been met has in part been born out of a myopic unwillingness to adapt the terms of cultural studies to suit the emergence of what I believe to be a wholly new intellectual climate. It is born out of an unwillingness to create new fictions and disciplines that can *challenge* the perpetual evacuation of meaning that Baudrillard has identified as the most significant feature of the 'postmodern condition'. This need not necessarily commit us to the elaboration of 'theoretical fictions' only capable of orbiting around the aporia that heralds the 'end' of theory. Instead we might look to, as it were, a 'fictional theory' that challenges not via the invocation of the discredited discourses that have accreted around the static notions of truth, history, the proletariate, etc. but rather a 'theory' that can operate obliquely, thereby being able to examine the fictions of postmodernity that when approached directly (*pace* Baudrillard) commit the text to a numbing spiral of uninflected irony, voiceless parody and the deadness of pastiche. That this is necessary, that new strategies have to be 'evolved', and that the work of Jean Baudrillard cannot simply be dismissed for perpetuating the sins of nihilism and fatalism and engendering a climate of cultural despair, can I hope be illustrated by examining the following two aspects of *contemporary* culture.

Baudrillard's writing found its cultural corrollary in two distinctive phenomena that were particular to the year 1988 in Britain: the emergence of 'Acid House' in music, its preeminence as both youth culture and dance craze, and the notoriety and success of the *Sunday Sport* as *the* British tabloid newspaper of the late 1980s. Both attest to the emergence of a new type of (de)sensibility which, detached from the gravitational pull of the real, now circulates within the imploded space of simulation. Within this space there are no hidden agendas to be unearthed by the cultural theorist – since there are no secrets. The old metaphors of excavation and penetration designed to legitimise the position of the critic have become empty postures in the face of the seamless surface of exposure and events in which everything is revealed with a pornographic clarity. It is a space that is unsympathetic to those who cling on to the old models of understanding – forcing them, as it does, away from explanation and into the ghetto of blind reaction and self-righteous indignation.

In this sense, neither of these two 'events' of 1988 can be understood without reference to the work of Jean Baudrillard and his account of postmodernity. However, the aim here is not to elevate these particular phenomena as the apocalyptic sealing of a fate or fatal tendency – they are symptoms rather than symbols of a culture in decline – but rather to demonstrate the shortcomings of those theoretical positions that fail to accommodate the changes in social space that postmodernism entails. For although we must resist the 'fatality' and negativity of the total implosion that Baudrillard describes, we must none the less discard those worn-out procedures and methodologies that are still tied to the rigidity of three-dimensional explicatory grids that *fix* meaning within the vectors of cause, time and effect. Neither 'acid house' nor the *Sunday Sport* offer themselves willingly to such analysis.

> Things have found a way to elude the dialectic of meaning, a dialectic which bored them: they did this by infinite proliferation, by potentialising themselves, by outmatching their essence, by going to extremes, and by obscenity which henceforth has become their immanent purpose and insane justification.
>
> Jean Baudrillard, *Les Strategies Fatales*

The 'Summer of Love (1988)' that the new 'acid' music heralded, emerged from a music industry already steeped in revivalism. 'Rare grooves', re-released funk and soul as well as synthetic or hybrid 1980s funk competed under the marketable sign of authenticity. What we witnesssed over the course of the year was an accelerating closure of the gap between the original and its retrossurection. Style, the most bankable asset of an otherwise barren music scene, had come to entail nothing more than the reworking of the antecedent. Ironically evidenced by the relatively new recording and play-back technology, it was clear that authenticity had become a question of surface – the scratches on a 'rare groove' being digitally recorded for a compact disc market that savoured the sign of the authentic recording over and above the vinyl actuality. The emergence of 'acid house' as a discernable musical genre in the spring of 1988 completed the ever-decreasing circle of revivalism – 'acid' being a mutated version of the Chicago house music introduced via Jack Master Farley's 'Love can't turn around' only eighteen months previously – and imploded the past into a permanent (and dancable) present. Relieved of the burden of authenticity and the debt to the pantheon of (male) authorial presences that centralised the cult of the personality within the history of rock, acid music emerged as a celebration not of 'His Master's Voice', but of the very *technology* that brought it into being.

The music itself occupies a new and peculiarly postmodern type of space – that of simulation. By continually reproducing its own means of (re)production – sequencing and sampling – it became like a reflexive utterance that is capable only of meditating upon itself. Favouring synchrony and the layering of form across the infinitely extendable surface of its reproduction, as opposed to the traditional diachronic or 'depth' model that leads the listener through the chorus and verse to a single founding (narrative) presence behind them, acid music, like much postmodern theory, could be characterised as free-floating, self-referential and hermetic. In specifically musical terms, it was like 'an electro-disco version of free-form jazz: weird repetitious sound textures and instrumental flour-ishes, mixed over bass-heavy drum patterns'.[6] However, what DJs termed the 'jack-virus' (unconsciously recalling Baudrillard's insistence that viral contamination is the only truly postmodern pathology) was in fact a specific drum rhythm of over 120 beats per minute, facilitated by the new technology of the digitalised 'beat-box'. The freneticism of the beat served cybernetically to 'suture' the various sound textures and different record-ings onto a single plane – an unrelenting but mesmeric surface. The syntactically complex 'language structure' of the 'song' in acid music is exchanged for the binary control of the beat which acts as a 'genetic code', microprocessing time by structuring and miniaturising each separate com-ponent of sound within a new reality based on the principle of digitalised equivalence. This is the technological reality that, in Baudrillard's words, 'is produced from miniaturised units, from matrices, from memory banks and command models – and with these it can be reproduced an infinite number of times ... It is nothing more than operational ... the product of an irradiating synthesis of combinatory models in a hyperspace without atmosphere.'[7]

If the form of the music followed the Baudrillardian description of a culture whose desires are to be found invested in new kinetic, numeric, fractal, artificial and synthetic images and sounds, so the response to it and the curious devotions of its cult following had similar resonances. The 'trance-dancing' that filled the 'acid' dancefloors could no longer be characterised within the traditional terms of expression and display. Rather it reflected a Dionysian abandonment to the beat that was both unselfconscious and oblivious – each individual dancer existing as a monad within the technological cocoon of an all-pervasive beat. Exhibi-tionist dance, based on the structuring of the body via the gaze, was no longer possible in the non-space of the acid house dance floor, which, like the more general non-space of postmodernism, failed to offer stable pos-itions or perspectives to which the 'look' could be anchored. Indeed the use of lowered ceilings, synthetic smoke, stroboscopic lighting and halluci-nogenic or semi-hallucinogenic drugs can be read as part of a self con-scious attempt to implode the traditional space of dance and public enter-tainment. In its place we witness a vertiginous and giddy neutralisation of the self and the determinations of the self to the 'code' – the digital inces-sance of the beat.

The euphoria that the acid phenomenon evoked amongst its devotees, gathered together under the seduction of the sign of 'Smiley' (the re-vitalised 1960s symbol of happiness) and the 'designer' drug ecstasy, cor-respond precisely with Baudrillard's diagnostic/prophetic account of the postmodern condition and sensibility to be found in *The Ecstasy of Communication*. In the following much-quoted passage he describes the 'ecstatic' celebration of the neutralisation of meaning in the supersatur-ated environment of 'information' technology:

We no longer partake of the drama of alienation, but are in the ecstasy of communication. And this ecstasy is obscene. Obscene is that which eliminates the gaze, the image and every representation. Obscenity is not confined to sexuality, because today there is a pornography of information and communication, a pornography of circuits and networks, of functions and objects in their legibility, availability, regulation and forced signification, capacity to perform, polyvalence, their free expression ...[8]

The 'ecstasy' that he describes finds its literal reading in the 'acid house' phenomenon. In the same essay Baudrillard analyses the forms of the 'ecstatic' pleasure that vitalised the new cult:

These no longer imply any game of the scene, the mirror, challenge or otherness; they are rather, ecstatic, solitary and narcissistic. Pleasure is no longer that of the scenic or aesthetic manifestation (*seductio*) but that of pure fascination, aleatory and psychotropic (*subductio*).[9]

Denunciations of technology as dehumanisation – the wedge that in splitting the self from the environment decentres the psyche, generating the sort of anxieties that fell under the modernist umbrella of alienation – in the context of acid house fail to account for this new and postmodern formation of pleasure. Instead technology is recast in the mould not of alienation, but of deliverance. Here, resistance appears as nothing more than an historical (modernist) conceit to an era which rewards submission with celebration.

Just as the music itself has been stripped of narrative, so too does the 'ecstasy of communication' that it invoked belong to a narrative or temporal vacuum. The various elements of the music, the 'sound textures' that slid across the surface of the drum-beat were therefore experienced as what Frederic Jameson terms 'pure material signifiers', no longer part of the narrative chain of the music's structure, available to the listener only as unrelated presents of time. Feelings were replaced by 'intensities' (Lyotard) that are mutable and free-floating. The 'ecstatic' response was therefore schizoid in character – the moods or intensities of the response being perfectly postmodern – alternating without contradiction between kitsch and dread, between the ecstasy of catastrophe and the terror of the simulacra.

Viewed as it were from the outside, through the representations and simulations to be found in the tabloid media, the 'acid house' phenomenon reflected a relationship between the media and the 'event' that is no less telling. Initially introduced by the *Sun* (1 October) as 'cool and groovy', the following few weeks brought a volte-face which resulted in a moral panic of epidemic proportions. What started off as an attempt to 'cash in' on a new but pre-existent youth culture – the *Sun*'s Bizarre Acid T-shirt offer – was quickly abandoned as the 'tabloid capital' of the phenomenon became apparent once the media controlled/induced panic was realised. The previously benign neo-hippy 'Smiley' motif of the *Sun*'s T-shirt offer changed signification overnight to become a 'sinister calling card' of hypnotic powers capable of sucking otherwise innocent white middle-class youth into the 'hellish nightmare' of the 'Killer Music'. A headline offensive followed, telling of evil and horror, calling for bans, linking acid music with international drug syndicates, rural rioting and, needless to say, aliens. As panic spread amongst an 'older generation', so interest was fuelled amongst those who were supposedly the source of that panic. The irony soon became clear. The very people who sustained the phenomenon as it spread from the urban centre (origination) to the rural peripheries were those (children/teenagers) whose understanding of it was entirely derived from its tabloid representations – representations that centred exclusively on scenes of drug-induced debauchery. Guidelines had effectively been established and a mode of behaviour assumed. The event by now had become self-generating and recursive and the media dream of raising up events by its very presence and coverage had been 'successfully' realised. It was perhaps another instance of the model (the prescriptive terms of panic) preceding the reality (the panic response) that it purports to describe.

Beckoning us from the margins of this technological landscape, Baudrillard invites us to cast away our doubts and join in, since he (with no shortage of assistance) has legitimised the party in the name of postmodernity. His philosophy, like the mesmeric beat of acid house, has no spaces or shadows for the sceptics to hide in, and asks us only to ignore the party-poopers and to submit to the beat – the rhythm of uninhibited consumption that is postmodernity. However, as Baudrillard continues to preside over the postmodern house, and 'simulation', like 'acid', becomes just another hackneyed party-cry, we might find ourselves beginning to question the nature of the celebration. After a while, we might suspect that the 'ecstasy of communication', like the trance dancing in the technological womb of the dance floor, merely cocoons us in a private and autistic world of our own. The beat may not stop, and the celebration appears to have no end. But that may be because the end is already here. After a while, we are left only with the 'ecstatic' smile that Baudrillard so tellingly describes: 'It is the smile that signifies only the need to smile ... like the Cheshire cat's grin it continues to float on faces long after all emotion has disappeared.'[10]

... the real is not only that which can be reproduced, but that which is already reproduced, the hyperreal which is entirely simulation.

Jean Baudrillard, *Simulations*

Warning: This is a REAL story about REAL people: But if you don't
believe it you can hear their tale by ringing our special number ...
Sunday Sport, 12 March 1989

The smile that crosses the faces of those who read the *Sunday Sport* 'newspaper' (assuming the term 'newspaper' still has some residue of meaning in
this instance), though different from the acid house party-goers, none the
less belongs to a facet of the same postmodern sensibility. The paper itself
follows many of the tabloid conventions already established by the Mur-
doch information empire, though it owes its existence to David Sullivan, a
porno-magazine publisher who bought it for a mere £150,000 and, after a
brief and unfortunate period of cross-fertilisation with the *Star*, raised its
readership to the present figure of approximately 600,000. It emerged, as
Stuart Wavell put it, writing for the *Guardian* newspaper, 'as a mammary-
bristling protozoan whose sense of editorial balance, one commentator
remarked, was making sure that its photographs showed both right and left
breasts'.[11] In this sense the *Sunday Sport* differs only quantitatively from
other tabloids such as the *Sun* and the *Star*, both of which have long been a
source of moral outrage and feminist indignation, but have not, needless
to say, nominated themselves as pertinent to an understanding of either
the 'postmodern condition' or the exegesis of that condition offered by
Jean Baudrillard.

Where the *Sunday Sport* differs radically from other tabloids, from here
on represented for the sake of convenience by the *Sun*, is that in hyperbolising tabloid conventions it has created a new media 'space'. It has
severed all ties to the plausible that had hitherto been the source of
'political' credibility. We learn from the *Sunday Sport*, for instance, that
not only is Hitler still alive, but so is Marilyn (now working as a nanny),
that mini UFOs are regularly mistaken for aspirin, that a woman has given
birth to a pensioner and, in perhaps the most celebrated headline to extend
the boundaries of orthodox conceptions of space and time: the 'World War
2 Bomber Found On Moon'.

None of this otherwise heady 'reportage' can really be said to lend itself
to the type of analysis traditionally advocated by the Left, which, following
the Althusserian model of ideology, bases its critique of the media on its
power to blinker the unspecified 'masses' from their (unspecified) but
none the less 'real' conditions of existence. In other words the *Sunday Sport*
refuses to conform to the traditional Left's preferred characterisation of
the socially irresponsible gutter press as the opiated fodder of an unin-
formed and lumpen proletariat. First of all, as the present editor of the
paper Drew Robertson points out, 'It's no longer your out of work
labourer. It's your City gent, your City whizzkid, who all find *Sunday Sport*
fun and a laugh.'[12] Secondly, and more significantly, it is extremely difficult, without patronising the readership out of existence, to see how *Sunday Sport* stories – for instance that of the Second World War bomber

found on the moon – can provide any alleviation from the harsh conditions of 'real' existence. For, although it would perhaps be possible, in a feat of intellectual gymnastics, to claim that the traumas of earthly existence might be offset by this almost utopian conception of lunar monotony broken by bits of bomber wreckage, it would stretch the limits of what might be termed plausible speculation to say the least.

Nor can the *Sunday Sport* be said to partake in the (nostalgic) myth of alienation, which conjunctively with ideology is the fulcrum of the social critique from the orthodox Left. Alienation, as we have learnt from this type of analysis, is a result of the contradiction between our technical mastery of the environment and the loss of personal autonomy that this mastery requires. However, for the *Sunday Sport*, the concept of alien(ation) takes on a wholly new set of connotative meanings, to do as much with UFOs and the (inevitably green) 'other' from outer space, as with any notion of social estrangement. Indeed, within the pages of the *Sport*, fear of the 'other' is often substituted for a sort of tingling delight and anticipation – the welcoming of an estrangement that is primarily sexual. The aliens in the *Sport* are brought into being mainly in order to inaugurate a new and sensational sexual morphology in the face of the bankruptcy of the tabloid's terrestrial terms of deviance and grotesquery. Even when aliens are cited without reference to their sexuality – as with the headline, 'Space Aliens Turned Our Son Into An Olive' – it is hard to map this onto the orthodox model of alienation as social estrangement. Instead we need to look at a new and 'postmodern' sense of 'knowingness', a willingly suspended disbelief in the play of fictions that can be distinguished from the cynicism and scepticism that was the legacy of a cultural era whose infallible deity circulated in the guise of rationality. It is a readership that refuses to become the duped 'mass' of a social theory that promises to speak on its behalf, but now must be reformulated and redefined within the terms of 'knowingness' and wilful participation.

The 'space' from which the *Sunday Sport* aliens emerge is neither the inner social space of investigative journalism, nor the outer space of traditional science-fiction, but literally 'the space in between the lines'. It is an intertextual space which, in shedding its mortgage to the real, appeals to the sort of ironic sense of play described above and also, perhaps more straightforwardly, a newly invigorated sense of the comic. In this perhaps most under-theorised aspect of postmodernism, the *Sunday Sport* is exemplary. Humour emerges in a form that is neither elitist (dependent on exclusion and the community of laughter that such exclusions entail), nor is it 'lumpen' in the sense of being without sophistication or subtlety. In fact it provides for a relatively sophisticated rereading and cross-pollination of the codes from which it derives – codes that are familiar to all, namely journalism and sci-fi. In this sense the humorous readings that it offers differ radically from those that one might attempt to extract from its sister tabloid the *Sun*. It is indebted far more to the type of humour propagated by a comic such as *Viz*, whose letters it almost exactly mimics in tone, and whose readership of dead-pan sophisticates once again hardly conforms to the type of sociological profile that allows the critic to indulge in the dismissal of whole sections of society as being deluded, duped, misinformed, alienated, estranged – or for that matter any other bracketting concept that is used to give form to the otherwise ineffable notion of the masses.

However, what the *Sunday Sport* does represent is an abandoning of the distinction between 'entertainment' and 'information' upon which the judgements of quality within journalism have traditionally rested. This tendency although not new, has intensified to the point at which the hype creates its own reality. The distinction made by Umberto Eco between what he terms 'paleo' and 'neo' TV, is here applicable to the world of newspaper/tabloid journalism: 'Its prime characteristic is that it [neo-TV] talks less and less about the external world. Whereas paleo-television talked about the external world, or pretended to, neo-television talks about itself and the contacts it establishes with its own public.'[13] In the light of Eco's analysis, the decline in journalistic standards capitalised upon by the *Sport* can not be reduced solely to the perniciousness of the circulation war, but must in some way take into account what he terms the 'contact' – or more appropriately in this instance, the contract – that it establishes with its readership.

The nature of this contract is touched upon by Dick Hebdige when he talks about the shifting ground that underlies the 'economy of truth'. According to the 'depth' model of analysis which attempts to excavate the truth from underneath the dissembling surfaces of appearance, the aliens that we learn about from banner headlines – Alien Baby Kept In Jam Jar, Aliens Turned My Son Into An Olive, etc. – could be regarded as, 'part of the ideology of authoritarian populism in which all aliens (e.g. gay men, the Loony Left, black youths, the IRA, acid house fans, etc.) are defined as a threat to the "family of the nation", as part of the unassimilable enemy within.'[14] However, as Hebdige is quick to point out, hidden agendas and conspiracy theories belong to a world in which information can still be organised and evaluated and hierarchised according to rigid structures of meaning. Mutations in the codes of journalism – codes that have until now acted as the guarantors of meaning – have with the *Sunday Sport* reached the stage at which they are no longer distinct from the 'information' that they promise to administer. They have, to use Baudrillard's term, become 'rituals of transparency'.

This transparency takes the form of an exorbitance of detail that is a familiar feature of pornography. But the *Sunday Sport* also pioneered and delivered to its readership a wholly new mutation of pornographic reality – alien pornography – soon recognised for its commercial potential and emulated by the other tabloids. Within the climate of 'journalistic' truth/reality already established, in which everything takes on the fascination of a sexual fetish, it was predictable, given that global politics were already being reformulated in terms of the protagonists' sexual appetites, that the encounter with the alien 'other' should also be a sexual encounter. The representational codes that determined journalistic possibility (printability) displace the old criteria, with its allegiances to truth and factuality, in a way that is globally imperial (everything being submitted, and reducible, to the results of the pornographic scrutiny) and sexually omnivorous. Regarding alien porn, this most recent manifestation of the encroachment of sexual fictionalising, Drew Robertson (the editor) stated that, 'If some woman is willing to tell you down the phone that she had sex with aliens, it is worth recounting to your readers.'[15] Under the new terms of information dissemination he has a point. But what is interesting about this shift is that it clearly indicates the emergence of a new and self-regenerative relationship between the media organ and its readership. More strongly it indicates a reflexivity that collapses the subject into the object – exactly the conditions for what Baudrillard describes as cold obscenity: 'Our obscenity is no longer palpable, it is transparent, it stretches past limits over the entire breadth of our communicational world. It is a cold obscenity, a bleached obscenity bereft of lubricity, of sensuality, of inhibition and of perversity. It corresponds to the insubstantiality of the real, and to its nullity.'[16] It also corresponds to a reevaluation of the contact (Eco) between the readership and their conception of (media) reality. In place of monogamous devotion to the 'real' we continually find new and ever more promiscuously virulent fictions, celebrated because they are, if nothing else, our own (re)creation. But as the celebration peaks with an orgy of extra-terrestrial copulation, there seems to be little room for self-congratulation.

From this point of view, the aliens that we know with such sexual intimacy on the pages of the *Sport* can be read as the ultimately ironic, hyperreal surrogates for our desires, in that they escape representation accross the ruined surfaces of the postmodern body. It is a body which, following Foucault, is an inscribed surface of events, which are both imprinted and destroyed by history. AIDS, the most vividly ravaging and distressing bodily surface, now becomes the metaphor for all breakdowns of immunity – not only those immune systems that separate the body from the outside, but those that separate fact from fiction, truth from falsity, reality from the imagination, paranoia from 'justified' fear and so on. In this sense the aliens may represent what Arthur Kroker describes in a different context as 'the ultimate out-of-body experience for the end of the world ... where the terror of the ruined surfaces of the body translates into its opposite: *the ecstasy of catastrophe and the welcoming of a sex without secretions as an ironic sign of our liberation.*'[17]

But in celebrating 'panic' (Kroker), in the apocalyptic terminology of the end of the world, we are forced to take the tendencies that are peculiar to postmodernism as *faits accomplis*. For although the *Sunday Sport* undoubtedly relinquishes the ability to distinguish between fact and fiction, truth and lies, it does so not in order to catalyse global crisis, but as a joke – a joke that is, needless to say, shared with all its readers (and maybe some of its commentators). It is a joke that could only take place within the context of postmodernism; a context in which blind faith in the legibility of the media and its power to guide us towards progress and enlightenment has already been lost. It is in this sense a 'game with the vestiges' of what preceded it. Alienation is now reconstituted as a joke rather than a history lesson, and aliens as sexual playthings – as enticement (without) as opposed to threat (within). The joke is just how far can we go before the illusion of control and mastery of the codes is lost? As Dick Hebdige points out, the potential dangers are also pretty clear: 'Today aliens from Mars kidnap joggers, yesterday Auschwitz didn't happen, tomorrow who cares what happens?'[18] But however we position ourselves in relation to this new problematic, it is clear that we cannot afford to ignore the claims made by Baudrillard. For the phenomenon of the *Sunday Sport* provides a more than adequate testimonial to the validity of his assertions regarding the 'logic' of contemporary culture:

> We are in a logic of simulation that has nothing to do with the logic of facts and the order of reasons. Simulation is characterised by *a precession of the model*, of all models around the merest fact – the models come first and their orbital circulation constitutes the genuine magnetic field of events. Facts no longer have any trajectory of their own, they arise at the intersection of models ... This anticipation, this precession, this short-circuit, this confusion of the fact with its model is what each time allows for all the possible interpretations, even the most contradictory – all are true, in the sense that their truth is exchangeable, in the image of the models from which they proceed, in a generalised cycle.[19]

It is a 'postmodern' logic which, as I have attempted to show, finds an uncanny correspondence in these two cultural phenomena: in the 'acid house' celebration of technology as delivering us from the mundane vicissitudes of lived experience, delivering us from the anguish of resistance to the ecstasy of cybernetic integration; and the *Sunday Sport*'s abandonment of the dialectics of meaning, of fact and interpretation to create a new and complicit manipulation of the codes in a paper that can only be described as more tabloid than tabloid. Of course neither of these two 'events' represent more than a tiny but none the less discernable 'tendency' to be found in the year 1990, nor are they reducible to a few purloined lines of Baudrillardian text. However, perhaps what they can do is convince the reader that the work of Jean Baudrillard is, despite the present critical climate, vital to an understanding of how we formulate 'the postmodern condition' – a problem that is approached through more orthodox texts in the next chapters.

Notes

1 Henri Lefebvre, *Everyday Life in the Modern World* quoted in Arthur Hirsh, *The French New Left: An Intellectual History from Sartre to Gorz* (South End Press, 1981).
2 See Zygmunt Bauman, 'Is There a Postmodern Sociology?' in *Theory, Culture and Society*, vol. 5, nos 2–3, June 1988.
3 Dick Hebdige, *Hiding in the Light* (Comedia, 1988), p. 191.
4 Dick Hebdige, 'A Report from the Western Front', *Block*, 12, 1986/87, p. 12.
5 See Jean Baudrillard, *The Evil Demon of Images* (Power Institute Publications, 1987) pp. 16–17.
6 Dave Snedells writing for *Time Out*, 1–8 June 1988.
7 Baudrillard, 'Simulacra and Simulations' in Mark Poster (ed.), *Jean Baudrillard: Selected Writings* (Polity, 1988) p. 167.
8 Baudrillard, *The Ecstasy of Communication*, Semiotext(e, 1987), p. 22.
9 Ibid., p. 25.
10 Baudrillard, *America* (Verso, 1988) p. 33.
11 See Stuart Wavell, 'The SS Storms Sunday', *Guardian*, 12 Dec 1988.
12 Ibid. quoted in *Guardian*.
13 Umberto Eco, 'A Guide to the Neo TV of the 1980s' in *Framework*, no.25.
14 Hebdige, 'After the Masses', *Marxism Today*, Jan 1989, p. 51.
15 Quoted in *Guardian* article.
16 Baudrillard, 'What are you doing After the Orgy?', *Artforum*, October 1983, p. 42.
17 Arthur and Marilouise Kroker, *Body Invaders: Sexuality and the Postmodern Condition* (Macmillan, 1988) p. 15.
18 Hebdige, 'After the Masses', p. 51.
19 Baudrillard, 'Simulacra and Simulations' in Poster (ed.) *Jean Baudrillard: Selected Writings*, p. 175.

2 Postmodernism: The Slippery Surface

Collapsing narratives

Rarely has the prefix 'post' generated such impassioned debate as now, when it is generally acknowledged that we inhabit an era that can, in some appropriate way, be characterised as postmodern. In an article published back in 1971, Brian O'Doherty indicated one possible cause of the intensity that surrounds the postmodern debate when he suggested that there might be 'an unconscious agreement to withhold a definition, partly because everyone's definition will expose the confusion the word is designed to cover'.[1] Such an agreement, whether conscious or unconscious, should not be dismissed as simply another episode in the history of cultural mystification. Rather, it can be understood as part of the contingent and discursive functioning that enables those discourses associated with postmodernism to throw into question the whole notion of the dominant that had hitherto been the distinguishing feature of modernist ideology. In other words, when viewed sympathetically, the semantic complexity of the term 'postmodernism', its ability to elude or withhold definition, testifies not to any lack of meaning but rather to the fact that meaning has been dispersed or redeployed across a much larger site of struggle and contestation. With this in mind, the following 'account' of postmodernism seeks to explore and elucidate the contours of the debate, the problematics and their 'lines of escape'.

Already we have come across an inversion of the traditional Anglo-Saxon analytical method. For in the context of postmodernism what becomes important and significant to the cultural theorist is no longer the moment at which the definition or sign is most congruent with what it is intended to circumscribe or refer to, but rather the moment at which definitions begin to crumble and the sign floats independently of the referent. The examination of *how* postmodernism is characterised is therefore important, not as a means of extracting ossifying definitions that are then consigned to the 'glass coffin' of cultural analysis, but in order to question the presuppositions of those of us who are anxious to rid the world of the new cultural 'other' – the 'post' that now calls into question modernist hegemony.

Of the three distinct but intrinsically interrelated elements by which postmodernism is commonly understood – as a particular type of textual practice or 'style', a cultural context and a mode of analysis – I shall in this section concentrate on the last two in order to demonstrate the impact that postmodernism has had on the production and consumption of all texts in contemporary 'first world' societies. For it is as a cultural context and mode of analysis that postmodernism most effectively problematises our critical assumptions about cultural production and subjectivity.

According to Dick Hebdige, the word postmodernism, 'if it signifies at all, announces at the very least a certain degree of scepticism concerning the transformative and critical powers of art, aesthetics, knowledge'.[2] And although Jean Baudrillard may presently represent the most corrosive voice of this scepticism, the critique of the way in which power is invested in these activities has been underway for at least two decades, in fact ever since feminists first began to develop new paradigms of social criticism which were no longer reliant upon traditional (patriarchal) philosophical underpinnings. It was under the umbrella of feminism and the feminist critique that, in the late 1960s and early 1970s, the various strands of what was to become known as the 'New Left' – Althusserian Marxism, semiotics and Lacanian psychoanalysis – were all drawn together in a process of cross-fertilisation and cross-theorisation. By the early 1980s this added up to a fairly well-established critique of 'master' narratives ('master' in the sense that they are both dominant and male) and to what Craig Owens has termed an 'apparent crossing of the feminist critique of patriarchy and the postmodernist critique of representation'.[3]

The nature of these 'master narratives' and the extent of the crossing of feminism and postmodernism has, over the past few years, been the subject of considerable debate.[4] For feminists, initially at least, they were specifically those narratives devised and told by men – in other words his/story – since this is the gender which has constituted itself as the subject of History. The crisis in Western representation, its authority (male) and its universalising claims, was thus a crisis that was first announced by those social groups that had been systematically denied historical representation. The feminist challenge to the patriarchal order of things was in this sense epistemological in that it questioned the structure of representations by interrogating the (male) system of legitimation by which they are endorsed or excluded. It was a challenge that aimed (literally) to give voice to hitherto marginalised or repressed discourses. In the present context, although the feminist interrogation of representation may undoubtedly appear to be the most significant, it is also important to heed Craig Owens' warning against either the forcing of a coalition of margins or the (re)presentation of the feminist challenge as monolithic.[5] To do so and to deny the multiple internal differences within the movement – essentialist, culturalist, Freudian, Lacanian, linguistic – is to deny the specificity of the feminist critique of patriarchy in an attempt to assimilate it within, rather than locate it as a part of, the more general postmodern critique of representation.

What is being documentated in a vague and sketchy way is the rise and fall of the modern myths of mastery and progress – myths that invariably take the form of narratives. Feminism is from this perspective the first significant assault on such mythology. In doing so it takes part in but also presages a more general collapse of faith in narratives that are not necessarily or exclusively gender specific. They are, according to Dick Hebdige, 'the Great Stories which for thousands of years the cultures of the West have been telling themselves in order to keep the dread prospect of otherness at bay.'[6] Postmodernism marks the decline of these 'Great Stories', of which he goes on to list just a few:

> ... divine revelation, the unfolding Word, the shadowing of History by the Logos, the Enlightenment project, the belief in progress, the belief in Reason, the belief in Science, modernisation, development, salvation, redemption, the perfectability of man, the transcendence of history through divine intervention, the transcendence of history through the class struggle, Utopia subtitled End of History ...[7]

So although feminism and postmodernism share common ground – they both present a critique of binarism, of thinking only in terms of exclusive oppositions and they both agree that the representational systems of the West admit only one vision, that of the constitutive male subject – they cannot be collapsed into one another simply on the grounds that they both attack 'metanarratives'.

To understand this we need to turn to the work of Jean-François Lyotard. In *The Postmodern Condition: A Report on Knowledge*[8] Lyotard presents a sustained critique of the modern investment of faith in the 'grand narratives' that have until now served to situate the activities of mankind – social, economic, political, scientific, religious, artistic – within broader metaphysical contexts. They are those overarching philosophies of history such as the Enlightenment view of the gradual but relentless progress of reason and freedom, Hegel's dialectic of the spirit coming to know itself, and perhaps most importantly Marx's drama of the forward march of human productive capacities via class conflict culminating in the just and revolutionary triumph of the proletariat.

The 'grand narratives' most important function is therefore that of legitimation. They serve to sanction certain activities (what have been termed 'first-order discursive practices'[9]) within a broader and totalising metadiscourse of legitimation, whilst withholding it from others. In doing so they function not just as selective filters but as epistemological frameworks without which 'man', the subject of history, is decentred and the 'universe' is committed to a new dark age in which chaos theory takes over from rationality and the Nietzschian vision of eternal return from the dialectics of Enlightenment. The metanarrative is thus in Lyotard's view 'meta' in the very strong sense noted by Fraser and Nicholson: 'It purports to be a privileged discourse capable of situating, characterising and evaluating all other discourses, but not itself infected by the historicity and contingency which render first-order discourses potentially distorted and in need of legitimation.'[10]

Within these terms the postmodern 'crisis' presents itself as exactly a crisis of legitimation. 'Our working hypothesis', writes Lyotard, 'is that the status of knowledge is altered as societies enter what is known as the postindustrial age and cultures enter what is known as the postmodern age.'[11] It is a transition that marks the end not just of an historical period mapped against, for instance, the development of capital (as per Ernest Mandel and later Frederick Jameson), but also the end of an entire age – of an entire way of life. The extent of this rupture was made glaringly explicit in an interview Lyotard gave in 1985. The postmodern is, he says,

> based fundamentally upon the perception of the existence of a modern era that dates from the time of the Enlightenment and that has now run its course: and this modern era was predicated on the notion of progress in knowledge, in the arts, in technology, and in human freedom as well, all of which was thought of as leading to a truly emancipated society: a society emancipated from poverty, despotism and ignorance. But all of us can see that development continues to take place without leading to the realisation of any of these dreams of emancipation.[12]

It is to scientific development, its justification and legitimation that Lyotard turns to demonstrate the most brutal declension of faith under the sign of the 'post'. The 'sorrow in the zeitgeist' that marks this sign can be attributed in large part to 'scientific' contributions to twentieth-century misery, the unbearable marriage of science and war (Virilio) – 'to write poetry after Auschwitz is barbaric' – the failure of science to make manifest the Utopia inherent in the modern narrative of Enlightenment, a narrative which it was presumed must culminate in emancipation. According to Lyotard there are two major forms of legitimation narrative, both of which must now be called into question. One is the narrative of emancipation, according to which people are the subject of science, and research undertaken by members of the general scientific community is justified in terms of the greater improvement of mankind as a whole. The other narrative takes not 'humanity' but the speculative mind or practice of philosophy, as the ultimate subject of science. 'Techno-science', to use Lyotard's term, is therefore autonomous in the sense that it is its own subject – any advancement in the totality of knowledge being in this sense self-legitimising. Neither of these two narratives now appears adequate in terms of justification.

The crisis of legitimation is therefore a breakdown in the belief that a unified totality of knowledge is either possible or desirable. It is a critique of the very idea of progress: 'One can notice a sort of decay in the confidence placed by the last two centuries in the idea of progress. The idea of progress as possible, probable or necessary was rooted in the certainty that the development of the arts, technology, knowledge and liberty would be profitable to mankind as a whole.'[13] Lyotard then proceeds to point out that despite disagreements, even wars, over the 'name of the subject' to be liberated, contestants have always been in agreement on the legitimacy of such activities, provided they could be conceptualised in terms of their eventual contribution to the liberation of mankind. 'After two centuries we are sensitive to signs that signify the contrary. Neither economic nor political liberalism, nor the various Marxisms, emerge from the sanguinary last two centuries free from the suspicion of crimes against mankind.'[14] Nor, needless to say, has modernism. Suspicions may not be focused on the atrocities to be found in the wake of the modernist movement, but they do none the less call into question (and even crisis) any belief in our ability to seek legitimation within the now somewhat soiled narratives of progress and enlightenment. They have, as it were, been 'exposed'. However, as a triumph of 'exposure' this is surely an empty victory, since there is no space for either congratulation or complacency. Rather we must confront the vital and pressing issue of where legitimation resides and how it is effected in a postmodern era.

Death of the author: whodunnit?

The scepticism that motivates Lyotard's critique of the 'grand' meta-narratives that have invigorated and legitimised the equally grand projects of humanism, can also be detected in the debate around the singular figure, the historical embodiment of humanism's grand ambitions – the author. Again it is a scepticism that is anti-teleological in its thrust, and which refuses to attach meanings to any 'founding' but invisible metaphysical presence that is, as it were, 'behind' those meanings. Forming a part of the same critique of the transcendent subject that Lyotard articulates in terms of the metanarratives of Enlightenment, Progress and Reason, the critique of the author is also an interrogation of 'man's' position as the centred origin and source, as well as the subject, of representation.

The two ideological narratives that we find fused in the modernist project and aesthetic are those of humanism and logocentrism. Both elements serve, at an ideological level, to divert attention away from critical analysis of the nature of the relationship between the political and the aesthetic. It is a diversion or subterfuge that appears to position the individual proposed by humanism in a very similar relation to the canonical painting of modernism. Both suggest autonomous beings possessed of self-knowledge, and an irreducible core of human or painted 'essence' that strives over history to perfect and realise itself. The term logocentrism, derived from Derrida, describes the tendency to refer all questions of the meaning of representations (novels, films, photographs, etc.) to a singular founding presence imagined to be behind them, be that author, history, *zeitgeist*, structure or any number of other bracketting concepts. Derrida, in disclaiming the transparency of language, its ability to escort the reader directly from words to meanings, forms a critique of the whole Western philosophical tradition as having been suffused with the 'metaphysics of presence' and founded on the privileging of speech over writing. His critique is equally applicable to the whole Western modernist tradition in the arts, in which meaning has been regarded logocentrically – as existing 'behind' the object/work of art, rather than fluctuating in and around its particular usage or cultural application.

It is in response to this theoretical climate, with its vitriolic denunciation of the primacy of the authorial presence, that much of the so-called 'progressive' artistic activity associated with postmodernism has been focused on the photographic or reproduced image. Although the mechanically reproduced image has not, as Walter Benjamin predicted it would,[15] been totally divested of 'aura', the photographic surface none the less offers little reassurance of the founding presence of the human subject. The absence of the brushmark or dribble that constitutes the index and trace of the expressive body, and of the human essence to which it plays host, therefore makes the photograph particularly resistant to appropriation within the authorial discourse of art history.

Much of the work that has taken place within this context is a literal re-enactment and visualisation of the 'death of the author'. Barbara Kruger who from the early 1980s has been montaging texts over appropriated photographs in using the shifting pronoun 'you' as her mode of address – 'Your fictions become history' – forces the (male) spectator away from the reassurance of being able to regress the meaning of the image back to a founding and stable presence behind it and finds himself instead positioning (him)self as the subject of the address, and the consumer of meaning. In another photo-text, Kruger combines the image of a woman wearing a hat with the declaration 'I am your reservoir of poses'. Commenting on the position of woman within the regime of representation, Kruger visualises the rites of exclusion that deny female authenticity and in its place allow only masquerade. Her examination of the construction of 'woman' through patriarchal language and its corresponding system of signs is interesting in that she does not create new speech so much as point to the need for a female voice whose lack is conveyed in her work – 'Your comfort is my silence'. This is significant in that it marks the so-called death of the author and by implication the death of authenticity as being gender specific. The funeral and the intellectual contestation of this death is therefore unsurprisingly predominantly male.

The work of Sherrie Levine confronts similar issues of authenticity, though this time within the more specific context of the history of art and artistic reproduction. Levine's recent work consists of rephotographed images taken from the history of the expressionist *avant-garde* – for instance the 'Horse' paintings by Franz Marc and the self-portraits of Egon Schiele. Reframed as photographs of already reproduced images, these images aim to expose the processes by which their otherwise hidden cultural agenda is transmitted and perpetuated. The language of expressionism is thus revealed in its specificity – in the Marc paintings, the ideological use of nature as the 'other', and in the Schiele portraits the mystifications of the psychobiological – as authentic in its own era but ideological in ours. By engaging with the simulacrum of the image, Levine shortcircuits expressionism's claims to a timeless transparency to reality and truth, premised as such a claim is on the historically specific discourses of originality and authenticity.

Epistemologically, art history has therefore always served to transmit a set of principles of authentication and a body of authenticated work. According to what has been the dominant view, the author discourse, works of art are identified as such in that they are seen to be the embodiments or depositories of an objectively discernible quality. Authenticity is a matter of this quality being traceable to its source in the individual author or creator. Artists, cultural-critics/commentators such as Kruger and Levine, are therefore engaged in photographic and reproductive techniques, because by their very nature they are distanced from this methodological approach. As Benjamin pointed out: 'to ask for the authentic print makes no sense.'[16]

Although the critique of the notion of the autonomy of the transcendental subject has been underway since Hegel's *Phenomenology of the Spirit*, it was not until 1968, with the publication of Roland Barthes' essay, 'The Death of the Author',[17] that this critique received any degree of recognition or critical attention within literary/theoretical circles. In an influential passage Barthes makes the following claims: 'We know now that a text is not a line of words, releasing a single "theological" meaning (the "message" of the Author–God) but a multidimensional space in which a variety of writings, none of them original, blend and clash'; 'the reader is the space on which all the quotations that make up a writing are inscribed without any of them being lost; a text's unity lies not in its origin but in its destination.'[18] Barthes' polemic is an example of what it describes. It extends the Foucauldian argument that the humanist subject 'man' is merely the product of the discourses of a particular moment (*The Order of Things*, 1966) and, following Derrida, dissolves the author into 'writing' which is seen to be the destruction of every voice and point of origin.

In 1969 Foucault re-entered the debate surrounding authorship with the publication of his highly influential text, 'What is an Author?', translated for the British journal *Screen* a decade later.[19] Here Foucault analyses the way in which the author is brought into existence as an ideological construction which serves to separate the text from its function within a particular set of (ideological) constraints. Although only one possible specification of the way in which a text functions discursively, the role assigned to the author – when compared to the relatively weak and shifting categories of, for instance, particular genres (romantic, horror, psychological, etc.), which also serve to map and determine the 'boundaries of the text' and therefore of meaning – is a role that seems to be a fundamental part of Western humanist/critical thought. It is also a role that is historically specific, since it must be underwritten by some sort of theory of expression or, as Foucault puts it, 'projection'. In this context he writes:

> Those aspects of an individual that we designate as an author (or which comprise an individual as author) are projections, in terms always more or less psychological, of our way of handling texts: in the comparisons we make, the traits we extract as pertinent, the conditions we assign, or the exclusions we practice.[20]

The degree to which these 'projections' have been naturalised within critical theory, is nowhere more evident than in the type of critical argument that takes place over whether this or that work is a masterpiece. Such argument can now be looked upon as being self-endorsing and utterly uncritical, since it cannot *fail* to benefit the status quo unless it succeeds in problematising the respective categories of 'work' and 'masterpiece'.

With regard to literary work, 'to only those books or texts with authors', Foucault identifies a number of different ways in which texts are owned and appropriated (according to inscribed copyright law and publishing procedure) and validated (usually according to what he terms 'author-function'). Most significantly, however, he makes the point that author-function is *not* formed spontaneously through the simple attribution of a discourse to an individual. Rather it results from a highly complex operation whose purpose is to *construct* a rational entity we can call the 'author'. It is an operation which, in the instance of this text for example, allows the reader to find stability within the precarious tissue of commentary, paraphrase, quotation, etc. by locating a single voice (that of the author) as predominant and also as capable of ordering the rising babble of secondary or competing texts.

So, within the 'plurality of egos' that constitute the text, that of the 'actual writer' is no longer seen to be determinate. We learn from Foucault that: 'Unlike a proper name which moves from the interior of a discourse to the real person outside who produced it, the name of the author remains at the contours of texts – separating one from the other, defining their form and characterising their mode of existence.'[21] By shifting critical focus away from the 'body' of the text towards its boundaries, the act of writing is now reconnected, in the Derridean sense, with that of disappearance, without the author-function also dissolving into the undifferentiated Barthian notion of *écriture*.

According to the humanist paradigm, the text points to a figure who is outside it and precedes it. Foucault deconstructs this notion of exteriority, positing instead that writing or image-making becomes merely the interplay of signs, regulated less by the content it signifies than by the very nature of the signifier. He writes, 'Thus the essential basis of this writing is not the exalted emotions related to the act of consumption or the isolation of the subject in language. Rather it is primarily concerned with creating an opening where the writing subject endlessly disappears.'[22] It is this process of 'disappearance' or slippage that, for Foucault, underlies the kinship between writing and death. For just as the Greek epic was designed to guarantee the immortality of the hero, so the grand narratives are seen as strategies for defeating death by positing a creative/expressive human essence that transcends the contingency of the subject. With the denial of the grand narratives writing becomes linked to the sacrifice of life and the voluntary obliteration of the self ... 'Where a work had the duty of creating immortality, it now attains the right to kill, to become the murderer of its author ... if we wish to know the writer in our day, it will be through the singularity of his absence and in his link to death which has transformed him into a victim of his own writing.'[23]

But, unlike Derrida, who regards this modernist self-erasure as a general condition of representation, Foucault takes issue with the notion that the author is conjured away in 'writing' to create a 'transcendental absence'. For as we have seen, in analysing 'author-function', he claims that the conditions for the discourse of 'man' and 'author' should be grasped in their historical specificity: '... the subject should not be entirely abandoned. It should be reconsidered, not to restore the theme of an originating subject, but to sieze its functions, its intervention in discourse, and its system of dependencies.'[24] One of the problems with Foucault's theory of discourse, as pointed out by Michael Newman,[25] is the opposition set up between a rigid discourse in which the subject is offered a position, and the amorphousness of subjectivity associated with, to use his example, the fluid desires of the body. Echoes of a similar problem are evident in the work of Lacan for whom the determinations of the 'law' become as rigid and unyielding as those of Foucaudian discourse. For Lacan, the process of birth-death being discussed occurs only with the subject's entry into the symbolic order: 'The subject is born insofar as the signifier emerges in the field of the Other. But by this very fact, this subject – which was previously nothing if not a subject coming into being – solidifies into a signifier.'[26] The (Oedipal) mechanisms that determine this process of solidification form the subject of chapters 5 and 6 are concerned specifically with the work of Lacan and of Deleuze and Guattari. Suffice it to say, for the moment, that the postmodern contestation of authorship, authenticity and originality has generated, and been generated by, an equally heated psychoanalytical contestation of subjectivity.

In crude terms, what is being described must be regarded as a substantial shift in the dynamics of cultural pathology. The alienated subject of modernism has been radically displaced from his or her position as founder of meaning. Representations (be they of the author or of the subject that the author wishes to (re)present) can no longer be tested against the real, as the real is itself constituted as everyday common-sense reality, in representations. In this sense, the metaphysics of modernism are no longer tenable. Distinctions between false consciousness and by implication 'true' consciousness and between the self and the 'other' are no longer available within the terms of a poststructuralist critique that jettisons the notion that there is any essential self preceding the social construction of the self. In Victor Burgin's words: 'The post-modern subject must live with the fact that not only are its' languages arbitrary, but it is itself an "effect" of language, a precipitate of the very symbolic order of which the humanist subject supposed itself to be the master.'[27]

Post-structuralism: a winner loses logic?

Implicit throughout the previous two sections has been the assumption that it is both possible and desirable to align an account of the 'postmodern condition' with the poststructuralist critique of metaphysics. In the following section I shall argue that poststructuralism, and specifically the poststructuralist critique of metanarratives (Progress, Enlightenment, Rationality) and metastructures (Author), is a vital part of any account of postmodernism that seeks to recognise it as a general cultural condition rather than as a set of artistic or stylistic practices. As a condition, postmodernism, as we have seen, throws into question the whole notion of dominance – dependent as it is on narrative hierarchies – thereby rendering its analysis, in terms of style alone, somewhat problematic. What distinguishes this condition is the *simultaneous* presence and coexistence of a number of different stylistic practices, none of which emerges as hegemonically dominant. Because of this, the version of postmodernism that is being narrated in this text is one in which poststructuralism is accorded the role of predication rather than merely presaging changes in cultural dynamics ordered under the sign of the 'post'.

The validity of such an assumption is appropriately illustrated by the widely accepted distinction between what Hal Foster has labelled a 'postmodernism of resistance' and a 'postmodernism of reaction'.[28] This latter neo-conservative critique of modernism, and of the particular moment of modernism associated with minimal and conceptual works, is of course a reactive one, since it proclaims, in their place, a return to history (the humanist tradition) and the subject (artist/writer) as master *auteur*. Of this position the critical writings of Hilton Kramer and the paintings of Julian

Schnabel are exemplary. Nothing could be further from the poststructuralist position which assumes the death of the subject not only as the
original creator of unique artefacts but also as the centred subject of representation and history; a position generally thought to constitute the 'progressive' face of postmodernism – Foster's 'postmodernism of resistance'.

It is a correspondence also articulated by Frederic Jameson who regards
the 'progressive' (for which we can read 'poststructuralist') account of
postmodernism as the only version capable of delineating the otherwise
uncolonised areas of aesthetics and experience:

> The contemporary post-structuralist aesthetic signals the dissolution of
> the modernist paradigm – with its valorisation of myth and symbol,
> temporality, organic form and the concrete universal, the identity of
> the subject and the continuity of linguistic expression – and foretells
> the emergence of some new, properly post-modern or schizophrenic
> conception of the artefact – now strategically reformulated as text or
> ecriture and stressing discontinuity, allegory, the mechanical, the gap
> between signifier and signified, the lapse in meaning, the syncope in the
> experience of the subject.[29]

The redefinition of the artefact, its historical passage from the modernist
'work' to the postmodern 'text', is therefore central to the problem faced
by the critical theorist. Whereas the 'work' is an aesthetic and symbolic
whole, sealed by an origin (the author) and an end (representative reality
or transcendant meaning), the 'text' is, to repeat Barthes, 'a multi-dimensional space in which a variety of writings, none of them original, blend and
clash'.[30] The stability of the sign as a unity of signifier and signified is lost in
the 'text' which reflects the dissolution of the sign and the released play of
signifiers. Within this pristine notion of textuality, in which the subject is
constituted in language alone, is the assumption that there is nothing
outside the text. Thus the search for and contestation of the 'truth' of
representations is no longer possible since it would be inconsistent to
defend the 'truth' of theoretical insights in a situation in which the concept
of 'truth' itself is part of the metaphysical baggage that poststructuralism
seeks to discard. With the erosion of the coordinates of value we enter into
what has been termed a period of post-criticism.[31]

Within the *modernist* ideology, the critic played a role analogous to that
of the author, in terms of the text's closure and anchorage to constructs
that exist only outside it. This connection also appears in Barthes' text,
'Death of the Author', when he points out that the conception of the
author, 'suits criticism very well, the latter then alloting itself the important
task of discovering the author (or its hypostasis: society, history, psyche,
liberty) beneath the work: when the author has been found, the text is
"explained" – victory to the critic. Hence there is no surprise that the reign
of the author has also been that of the critic.'[32] In this light the function of

the critic has been analogous to that of the author. Both serve to end doubt concerning meaning (and therefore worth) through a process of closure – establishing boundaries within which the text can be contained. In this way criticism offered the reassuring security of an explanation as well as an evaluation. But, more significantly, it is argued that criticism functioned to return the reader from the uncomfortable and precarious position of producer of meaning to the easier position of consumer.

Although the exclusion of the individual from engagement with the production of meaning and the subsequent emphasis on his/her existence within the increasingly closed cycle of consumption must be one of the truly distinguishing features of our postmodern/late capitalist environment, the poststructuralist notion of pure intertextuality *fails* to reinstate the viewer/reader as producer of meaning. The text, which is constituted as endlessly proliferating meanings with no stable points of origin or closure, denies the reader privileged access to any part of it. Therefore, although he or she may, as it were, occupy a position as producer of meaning – the act of consumption now being treated as a productive (active) process – this position is itself an empty one. Although the reader/consumer creates and produces meaning, (s)he can only do so in a way that is instantly self-abolishing. Paradoxically, the moment at which meaning is 'produced' is therefore the same moment at which it is denied. The stability that it suggests (a perspective, point of view, a position, etc.) is illusory (a simulation), as there is no 'outside' from which the act of consumption can become productive and meaningful. Instead there is only the closed (poststructuralist) code of equivalence – a code in which the reader/consumer circulates endlessly, condemned to a perpetual motion.

This is at least the 'vulgarised' form that poststructuralism is forced to assume by its critical opponents who seek to reduce a multi-dimensional theoretical position to a single homogeneous entity, capable only of reducing the 'great' humanist achievements to undifferentiated *écriture*. None the less, as a critical procedure, poststructuralism demands careful formulation if it is to avoid what Jameson describes as the 'winner loses' logic of the totalising dynamic. He goes on to say:

> What happens is that the more powerful the vision of some increasingly total system or logic – the Foucault of the prisons book is the obvious example – the more powerless the reader comes to feel. Insofar as the theorist wins, therefore, by constructing an increasingly closed and terrifying machine, to that very degree he loses, since the critical capacity of the work is thereby paralysed, and the impulses of negation and revolt, not to speak of those of social transformation, are increasingly seen as vain and trivial in the face of the model itself.[33]

Spectacle and code: falsification or neutralisation?

Many aspects of the totalising system de- and then re-constructed within
the terms of the poststructuralist critique are evident in the writings of
Debord and Baudrillard. Debord's *Society of the Spectacle* opens with a
quotation from Feuerbach: 'our time prefers the image to the thing, the
copy to the original, fancy to reality, the appearance to essence.'[34] Debord
then proceeds to characterise late capitalist society as one in which both the
image and the subject have been transformed according to a pervasive
process of commodification. Everything now exists only in representation,
staged in its commodified form as 'spectacle'. This, for Debord and the
other 'Situationists', represents not just another phase in the 'evolution' of
capital but a wholly new set of social relations built around the 'spectacle'
which asserts the primacy of sight and the gaze in place of capital's previous
attachment to use and value. It is as if the retina itself has been commodified and conscripted to the service of capital.

Recognising that it is no longer as producers but as consumers that our
consciousness is formed, Debord suggested that the 'commodity society'
that we inhabited in the 1950s had by the late 1960s metamorphosed into
the 'Society of the Spectacle'. It is a society that offers no experience of
'reality' that is not mediated by capitalist ideology, since it is a society that
simultaneously meets our needs whilst producing our consciousness
through a web of ideologically coercive 'spectacles'. Debord describes this
unilateral process of commodification in relation to the image, around
which society and social relations are now organised and preserved: 'The
image has become the final form of commodity reification . . . the spectacle
is capital to such a degree that it becomes the image.'[35] The transmutation
of the thing into the image is now regarded as the specific result of a concrete
historical moment in which the economy, developing internally and autonomously, reproduces its conditions of production. It represses the value of
use under the elevation of that of exchange; 'Its mechanical accumulation
liberates an unlimited artificiality . . . The accumulative power of an independent artificiality leading everywhere to a falsification of social life.'[36]
Implying the death of experience in which codes and operative processes
become replacements for natural law, Debord describes a consumer culture defined by appearance; the wordless communication of consumption
and the fetishisation of merchandise according to the mechanisms of distance, desire and the domination of the code.

Like Debord, Baudrillard attacks the dualities of the real and the representational and of truth and falsity. However, where Debord maintained
the paradoxical belief that separation is itself part of the unity, that the
limits between the false and real have been effaced by the repression of all
lived experience under the very *real* presence of falsity, Baudrillard an-
nounces the abolition of the spectacular and therefore the very idea of
falsity. The spectacle now becomes simulation.

Defining simulacra as copies for which there are no originals, Baudrillard makes the well-known claim that 'The very definition of the real has become that which it is possible to give an equivalent reproduction ... The real is not only that which can be reproduced , but that which is already reproduced ... The hyperreal ... which is entirely simulation.'[37] Hyperreality is defined as the circuiting of codes rather than of meaning, within a closed system of symbolic exchange – the absolute form of the code circuiting free from its referent, its objective reality or material alibi. In such self-regulating systems the signifier becomes its own referant, in tautological repetition of itself. Baudrillard writes that the era of simulation,

> begins with the commutability of terms that were once contradictory or dialectically opposed ... In politics of the left and the right, in the media of true and false, in objects of utility and uselessness, and of nature and culture on the very level of signification. All the great humanist criteria ... have been effaced in our system of images and signs. Everything has become undecidable – this is the characteristic effect of domination by the code, which rests on the principle of neutralisation and indifference.[38]

The irony of contemporary (postmodern) existence is, therefore, that what we accept as reality is already simulated, a massive fabrication of effects that stand in for reality's absence.

Although the two formulations of postmodernity, Debord's 'society of the spectacle' and Baudrillard's 'society of simulation', share common ground – both describe the 'crisis' of representation that informs the post-structuralist critique of 'meaning' – they none the less remain distinct. The 'spectacle' described by Debord, although ideologically coercive, is still a possible site of (political) intervention. It is *staged* and assimilated according to a gaze that distances and objectifies – in other words it still belongs to a dialectical epistemology that counterpoises a fixed notion of reality with one that is distantiated, alienated or estranged by the various operations of capital.

> Thus [writes Baudrillard] consumer society lived also under the sign of alienation, as a society of the spectacle. But just so: as long as there is alienation, there is spectacle, action, scene. It is not obscenity – the spectacle is never obscene. Obscenity begins precisely when there is no more spectacle, no more scene, when all becomes transparence and immediate visibility, when everything is exposed to the harsh and inexorable light of information and communication.[39]

This is the 'society of simulation' in which there is no theatre because there is no longer any stage upon which it could be performed. Instead of the lingering representational narratives that inspired the 'Situationist' aggravation of the 'spectacle', we find only a blank supercession of unrelated events on the flat, depthless surface of the postmodern screen.

The system described by Baudrillard is therefore total, precluding notions of either critical intervention or political agency. The binary schema of question and answer renders inarticulate every discourse. In terms of artistic activity, attempted interventions through the use of image appropriation and montage – such as the work of Barbara Kruger or Sherrie Levine discussed earlier – function merely to reinforce the hegemony of the code. Within the Baudrillardian analysis, montage and codification demand, in effect, that the viewer construes and decodes by observing the same procedures whereby the work was assembled. The reading of the message is thus reduced to a perpetual examination of the code. To quote Baudrillard again:

> Every message is a verdict, just like the one that comes from the polling statistics. The simulation of distance (or even of contradiction between the two poles) is only – like the effect of the real that the sign seems to emit – a tactical hallucination.[40]

Bereft of spatial coordinates and therefore the notion of critical distance, practices of cultural resistance and political/cultural intervention are secretly disarmed and reabsorbed by a system of which they themselves form a part, since they can achieve no distance from it. Ironically, this applies to the Baudrillardian text as well as the culture of simulation that he sets out to describe. Thus in many ways Baudrillard becomes the self-appointed sophist of poststructuralism – as the culture and text that he describes as descriptive medium implode into one another on the single plane of simulation.

Rupture or continuity

Any overview that attempts to run through Lyotard's critique of the 'grand recits' or modernist metanarratives, Foucault's contestation of authorship, Barthes' interrogation of the operations of criticism, Debord's account of the transformation of the thing into the image and Baudrillard's final demolition of all authenticity (progressive, authorial, critical or spectacular) into the undifferentiated realm of simulation, lays itself open to the twin charges of conflation and generalisation. Lengthy exegesis and the critical elaboration of these accounts of the various facets of the postmodern problematic have, for the purposes of this chapter, been discarded. Instead, I have imposed an epistemological unity that could provide the basis for a 'general theory' of postmodernism. For, although the relationship between Lyotard, Foucault, Barthes, Debord and Baudrillard is, to say the least, strained, they can be said to meet on common theoretical ground – the ground of poststructuralism.

All these 'theories' regard the decline of nature as being causally linked to the decline of the signified, or referant, as guarantee of objective truth, from which comes the deconstruction of the transcendental subject as the origin or source of meaning. All observe the demise of structures of interiority that underly the humanist paradigm. In this sense postmodernism is constituted as a direct reflection of the breaking down of what Marcuse termed the 'semi-autonomy of the cultural sphere'. And although viewed positively we can say that this allows the image to circulate in a wider semiotic environment (the image as per Debord now having penetrated every enclave of private as well as public life), the search for the 'truth' of representations becomes irrelevant, and all that we are left with is an interrogation of its effects. Poststructuralism most clearly articulates this, attesting as it does to the erosion of those coordinates of value that under modernism had anchored the critique or theory in a stable relation to its object.

Such a process of erosion does not, however, take place within a vacuum, nor does it leave a void. What is being witnessed is undoubtedly a liquidation of the modernist ideology's claims to homogeneity and univocality, although we could still ask whether or not such claims should be identified as being particular to the (historical) age of modernism, or to the age of its analysis. In other words, postmodernism constructs modernism as its cultural 'other' only through an imposed post-rationalising in which it is falsely reconstituted as being 'homogeneous and univocal'. The danger here is that when theoretical discourse (of any sort) comes under the label of postmodernism it tends to get sucked into the orbit of the kind of discourse that emphasises radical rupture and discontinuity; the very type of dichotomous thought patterns that Derridean deconstruction urges us to abandon.

A number of questions emerge. Does, for instance, the critical discourse that addresses itself to postmodernism actually act as a blockage to the modernist power mechanism that had operated unchallenged up to that point, or is it not in fact part of the same historical network as the thing that it denounces? Equally, is there really an historical rupture between the age of modernism and its critical analysis? If not, then is not postmodernism, rather than being a new episode in the lessening of the modernist monopoly, simply a more devious and discrete form of the same power?

In an article published in the journal *New German Critique*,[41] Andreas Huyssen attempts to address some of these issues. Following a persuasive but ultimately unproductive line of thought, Huyssen argues that the poststructuralist critique is, in fact, more continuous with modernist ideology than many of its apologists are prepared to admit. His claim is based on a literal reading of Derrida's claim regarding the reflexive nature of language, that, 'we cannot legitimately transgress the text towards something other than it, towards a referent (a reality that is metaphysical, historical, psychobiological, etc.) ... There is nothing outside the text.'[42] Such a pristine notion of textuality has, in Huyssen's words, led to 'the privileging of the aesthetic and the linguistic which aestheticism has always promoted to justify its imperial claims.'[43] Significantly, the list of no-longer-possibles – realism, representation, history, etc. – corresponds closely to that of high modernism. Though not the modernism of alienation and negativity, the playful transgression of the post-structuralist position articulated by Huyssen is a modernism which, in its absences and deferrals, produces not anxiety but 'jouissance' and a modernism of critical affirmation.

In this way it is claimed that poststructuralism attacks the appearance of late capitalist culture but misses its fundamental features. Differences in practice are subsumed under the monolith of 'textuality' and important distinctions are forfeited. For, if poststructuralism is to distinguish itself from the 'reactionary' ideology of modernism, it must be able to reflect the breakdown of traditional languages that are reconstituted in different ways. By formalising the poststructuralist position as simply a 'textual' denial of subjectivity, Huyssen attacks it on the grounds that it jettisons the chance of challenging the ideology of the subject by developing alternative and different notions of subjectivity. Thus the poststructuralist decentring of the subject, the disentrenchment of representation and the erosion of the sense of history and the referent is seen only in terms of its rejection of the question of who is speaking. This, in his own words, 'merely duplicates on the level of aesthetics and theory what capitalism as a system of exchange relations produces tendentionally in everyday life: the denial of subjectivity in the very process of its construction'.[44] Poststructuralism is therefore articulated purely negatively, in terms of its collusion in the schizophrenic collapse of the subject and of historical narrativity, both of which are lamented rather than celebrated as signs of the same process of fragmentation and reification under late capitalism. If this was indeed the case, then the poststructuralist critique itself would have to be treated as a symptom rather than a methodological predication of postmodernism. To do so would not only involve misrepresentation, but would also forfeit the radical possibilities, in both praxis and theory, that such a position offers.

Huyssen's critique of poststructuralism as a philosophy of textual aestheticism is based on the reduction of a complex and heterogeneous set of propositions to a single deconstructionist aspect, captured and sloganised with Derrida's claim that, 'there is nothing outside the text'. However, what Derrida is proposing is not some new and more comprehensive critical doctrine, or dogma, but rather a problematisation of any theory of knowledge that claims to escape the reflexivity of language. Nietzsche, who must be regarded as Derrida's philosophical forefather, adopts a similar position whilst at the same time he indicates how we hide from the implications of this claim: 'We cease to think when we refuse to do so under the constraint of language; we barely reach the doubt that sees this limitation as a limitation.'[45] What is at stake is the issue of 'representation', specifically the object of study in the critical text, and what is being challenged is the view that any definitive theory is possible. This challenge is itself reflexively paradoxical and applies as much to the poststructuralist critique itself as it does to the initial object of that critique. Thus, to claim as Huyssen does that all differences of practice are subsumed under the monolith of 'textuality', is to take the poststructuralist critique to be exactly the sort of 'definitive', all-encompassing theory that it paradoxically refuses to be.

The poststructuralism that emerges is not only incompatible with the concept of structure, it is also radically anti-scientific. The view of criticism as an operation performed by a self-possessed subject upon a discrete and distanced object is discarded. Instead, as we learn from Barthes, criticism becomes an act of reading – imbricating and implicating a divided and unstable subject into the multiple instabilities of a text that continually opens onto other texts. Barthes writes:

> it is part of the theory of the text to plunge any enunciation, including its own, into crisis. The theory of the text is directly critical of any metalanguage: revising the discourse of scientificity, it demands a mutation in science itself, since the human sciences have hitherto never called into question their own language, which they have considered as a mere instrument.[46]

Unlike traditional theoretical 'positions' (structuralism included) which are created in order to provide stable reference points from which the instruments of analysis can appear to function autonomously, independent of their various manipulations, poststructuralism offers no 'position' which is not in some way self-abolishing. For this reason, detailed observational analysis and extended explicatory grids are discarded in favour of instantaneous flashes of paradoxical illumination that are resistant to co-option within (static) epistemic systems. What is important is that with the destruction of the traditional stance of objectivity and the traditional goal of truth, scientific knowledge becomes less valuable than artistic, literary or political activity. This is something that seems to have been largely forgotten as poststructuralism has become institutionalised as a 'theory' of literary deconstruction. By concentrating on the work of Deleuze and Guattari in later sections of this book, I hope to redress this imbalance by returning the ambition of the poststructuralist critique towards this imperative to artistic, literary or political activity.

The poststructuralist suspicion of comprehensive and unifying structures corresponds directly to Lyotard's account of the postmodern condition in terms of the demise of the great narratives of legitimation, and the emergence of some 'new', and as yet virtually untheorised, form of subjectivity. What poststructuralism offers is a more appropriate means of articulating this so far uncharted territory. In holding up a mirror to contemporary processes of fragmentation, temporal dislocation and subsequent loss of identity, it aims to relocate the 'natural' descriptive vocabulary for our contemporary culture of advanced consumer capitalism. This vocabulary is dependent on an ability to distinguish between two possible modes of functioning for the sign. The mode analysed by the structuralists and semioticians is conventional in the sense that the sign, and the meaning that it generates, is seen to work rigidly, despotically and predictably. On the other hand, there is the unconventional mode where the sign works creatively, anarchically and irresponsibly. This, according to the poststructuralists, is the mode that represents the 'real' being of the sign. In its 'real' being, therefore, the sign no longer reinforces; it subverts controlled systems of every kind. In examining the way that this process of subversion is characterised, the symptoms of the sign as it functions anarchically in a way that escapes its domestication within systems of meaning, the next chapter aims to establish the nature of the general resistance to postmodernism as it has so far been described.

Notes

1 Brian O'Doherty, *Art in America*, May/June 1971, p. 19.
2 Dick Hebdige, 'A Report from the Western Front', *Block*, 12, 1986/7, p. 10. For an extended discussion of the issues raised in this article see Hebdige, *Hiding in the Light* (Comedia/Routledge, 1988).
3 Craig Owens, 'The Discourse of Others: Feminists and Postmodernism' in Hal Foster (ed.), *Postmodern Culture* (Pluto, 1985).
4 See Owens as above, Barbara Creed 'From Here to Modernity – Feminism and Postmodernism, *Screen*, vol. 28, Spring 1987, and Nancy Fraser and Linda Nicholson's 'Social Criticism without Philosophy: An Encounter between Feminism and Postmodernism', *Theory, Culture and Society*, vol. 5, Nos 2–3, June 1988.
5 See Craig Owens, 'The Discourse of Others: Feminists and Postmodernism'.
6 Hebdige, 'A Report from the Western Front', p. 10.
7 Ibid., p. 11.
8 Jean-François Lyotard, *The Postmodern Condition, A Report on Knowledge* (Manchester University Press, 1984).
9 This term is derived from Fraser and Nicholson's analysis of Lyotard in 'Social Criticism without Philosophy: An Encounter between Feminism and Postmodernism'.
10 Ibid., pp. 376–7.
11 Lyotard, *The Postmodern Condition*, p. 3.
12 Lyotard interview with Bernard Blistine, 'A Conversation with Jean-François Lyotard', *Flash Art*, no. 121, March 1985.
13 Lyotard, *Postmodernism*, ICA Documents, 4, 1986, p. 6.

14 Ibid., p. 6.
15 See Walter Benjamin, 'The Work of Art in the Age of Mechanical Reproduction' in *Illuminations* (Jonathan Cape, 1970).
16 Ibid., p. 226.
17 Roland Barthes ' The Death of the Author' in *Image, Music, Text* (1977).
18 Ibid., p. 149.
19 See Michel Foucault, 'What is an Author?', *Screen*, Spring 1979.
20 Ibid., p. 21.
21 Ibid., p. 19.
22 Foucault, *Language, Counter-Memory and Practice* (Cornell University Press, 1977) p. 136.
23 Ibid., p. 137.
24 Ibid., p. 137.
25 Michael Newman, 'Revising Modernism, Representing Postmodernism' in *Postmodernism*, ICA Documents 4, 1986.
26 Jacques Lacan, *Four Fundamental Concepts of Psychoanalysis* (Peregrine, 1986), p. 199.
27 Victor Burgin, *The End of Art Theory: Criticism and Postmodernity* (Macmillan, 1986), p. 49.
28 See Foster (ed.), *Postmodern Culture*.
29 Frederic Jameson, *Fables of Aggression* (University of California Press, 1979), p. 19.
30 Barthes, 'Death of the Author' in *Image, Music, Text*, p. 146.
31 See Gregory Ulmer, 'The Object of Post-Criticism' in Foster (ed.), *Postmodern Culture*.
32 Barthes, 'Death of the Author', p. 147.
33 Frederic Jameson, 'The Cultural Logic of Late Capitalism', *New Left Review*, no. 146, July/Aug 1984, p. 57. Also published in abbreviated and revised form in Foster (ed.), *Postmodern Culture*.
34 Guy Debord, *Society of the Spectacle* (Red and Black, 1983).
35 Ibid.
36 Guy Debord, *Society of the Spectacle* (Rebel Press, AIM, 1987), section 68.
37 Jean Baudrillard, *Simulations*, (Semiotext(e), 1983), p. 146.
38 Baudrillard, *L'Exchange Symbolique et la Mort* (Gallimard, 1976) p. 21. Part of this essay is reprinted in translation in Mark Poster (ed.), *Jean Baudrillard: Selected Writings* (Polity, 1988).
39 Baudrillard, 'The Ecstasy of Communication' in Foster (ed.), *Postmodern Culture* p. 130, also published in full by Semiotext(e) 1988.
40 Baudrillard, 'Simulations', p. 117.
41 See 'New German Critique', *Modernity and Postmodernity*, no. 33, Fall, 1988.
42 Jacques Derrida, *On Grammatology* trans. Gayatri Spivak (Johns Hopkins University Press, 1976) p. 158.

43 *New German Critique* p. 44.
44 Ibid., p. 47.
45 Frederick Neitzsche, *Will to Power*, trans. Kauffman/Hollingdale (Vintage Books, 1968) sec. 522.
46 Roland Barthes, 'Theory of the Text' p. 35 in R. Young (ed.), *Untying the Text* (Routledge and Kegan Paul, 1981).

3 Semiology, Meaning and Aesthetics

The structuralisms and poststructuralisms outlined in the previous chapter provide the epistemological framework against which a more general awareness of 'postmodernism' has been profiled – an awareness of what might be termed a 'postmodern aesthetic'. What has emerged over the past few years is not so much a redefinition of the aesthetic, but rather a more general consensus of opinion pointing to a decline of faith in the *transformative* powers of the arts – in the plausibility of distinctions between art and advertising, traditionally cast in terms of distinctions between high and low, or authorised and popular culture (unauthorised in the sense of being without discernible pedigree or genealogy). That corresponds almost exactly to Lyotard's claim that we have entered a cultural phase in which *creative* as well as political effort has been cast adrift from the moorings and legitimations of the grand narrative structures. It is a phase marked by a new sort of promiscuity in which the various strands of human activity jostle, intermingle, and exchange amongst one another. With the loss of their respective Gods (the 'metas' of the narratives), sovereignty is lost and 'art', like advertising, becomes answerable no longer to itself – thereby preserving the myth of autonomy – but to the vicissitudes of the market place. It is an 'aesthetic' that therefore corresponds to the loss of the privileged sign. For in the semiotic 'Brownian' broth of postmodernity it might well appear that it is no longer possible to distinguish the aesthetically impregnated sign of 'art' from the sign of 'life'. Neither willingly admits meaning, other than that meaning inherent in the act of their consumption, and both submit to the blankly postmodern aesthetic of fascination. And yet, the debates surrounding the issues of postmodernism are at their most popular, as well as heated, when they are regarding 'art' . . . a category whose very fate might appear to be already determined.

It is as an attempt to unravel this paradox that this chapter examines the way in which recent art production has been characterised and considers its relationship to the wider semiotic environment in which it must now circulate and to the discipline of semiology which has displaced that of traditionally defined 'art history' as the predominant mode of understanding (and meaning). By addressing the four paired terms, meaning and semiology, aesthetics and art-history, and the cross relationships and exclusions that these terms establish, it aims to provide a reading of post-modernism in terms of the categorisation of images. However, it is a question that is raised not through the examination of art works themselves and the validity of their claims to be in some way appropriately post-modern, but rather by looking at those discourses and narratives of legitimation that serve to effect the distinction between the 'aesthetic', 'the semiotic' and the 'real'.

In 1985, after six months at the New Museum of Contemporary Art in New York, an exhibition called simply the 'Difference' exhibition was staged at the Institute of Contemporary Art in London. Accompanying lectures aimed at providing a theoretical exegesis of the exhibited works' engagement with the issues of 'postmodernity'. With the exception of the films, all the work exhibited adopted the format of the photo-text. Much of the work played upon and even referred directly to the translated texts of French writers engaged with the issues of ideology and representation – most notably Althusser, Barthes, Derrida, Foucault, Lacan and Kristeva. Nearly all of the work displayed sought to deconstruct representational strategies according to models of meaning directly inherited from semiology and semiological methods of understanding. The fervour with which this was pursued suggested the emergence of a new (and perhaps post-modern) faith – if not art. Radicalism and even marginality were the keynotes sounded in 1985, though we can now look upon the work as belonging to a new orthodoxy of 'postmodern' production bound to the politics of media representation and a defiant belief in the deconstructive political power of the semiological method.

But despite the diligence of intention and ideological rigour of the work displayed – a tightening of the belt in the face of the political/ideological flabbiness of the concurrent strand of neo-expressionism in painting – there was an air of *tristesse* that permeated the exhibition and the accompanying talks. With hindsight, it seemed to centre on the unvoiced and nostalgic suspicion that overtly de/reconstructive visual strategies can never in themselves constitute good art. But as the exhibition relentlessly insisted, 'art' had *died* at the hands of semiology, to be dispersed across a number of different 'media' practices. This was being celebrated, however, not because it signalled the end of an archaic and politically reactionary institution, but rather because it had allowed 'art' to emerge like a phoenix in exactly the absoluted and inviolable form that the critique appeared to deny. (We shall return to the function of semiology in relation to this sort of paradox at the end of this chapter.) To begin with, however, we must continue to look at the way that postmodernism has been constituted *within* the 'art-world'.

Appended to Peter Wollen's essay, 'Counter Cinema and Sexual Difference',[1] which was part of the critical text that comprised the 'Difference' exhibition, there are three lists under the headings, 'Films',

'Cinematic Contexts' and the 'Extra-Cinematic'. These lists supposedly document the trajectory of postmodernism in its different forms from 1970–8. Appearing strangely idiosyncratic in a collection of texts that itself constitutes a critique of historical narration, their inclusion appears to be part of a hitherto neglected attempt to chart the evolutionary topography of the discourse of postmodernism. Ignoring the interesting narrational gap between 1978, the last documented date, and the publication date of 1985 – did the discourse of 'Difference' stop in 1978, perhaps under the sinister spectre of Baudrillardian indifference, or was it superseded by the more marketable discourses of 'Desire', 'Subjectivity' and 'French Theory' that crowded the ICA agenda in the following years? – the composition of the list itself is worthy of attention. Of the twenty-eight entries under the heading 'The Extra-Cinematic' – for Wollen constituted the key historical moments of the discourse (of difference) with which the exhibition was ostensibly engaging – only two entries, Mary Kelly's 'Post-Partum Document' (1976), and Victor Burgin's Eindhoven exhibition of the following year, can be considered to belong to the corpus of work which, traditionally at least, has looked towards an establish(ment)ed 'art-world' for legitimation. Conjecturally, we might regard the form of the list as suggesting either that 'theory' itself has become an art-form (or at least an adequate substitute for absence of fine art) or alternatively, that the dispossessed discipline of art-history has been replaced by that of media analysis, even though the institutional terms of its propagation, and maybe even its audience, appear to have remained the same. Either way, the space of displacement is not an empty one.

Returning to Wollen's list. Starting in 1970 with the publication of Juliet Mitchells' influential text *Why Freud?*, Wollen's historiography (hagiography?) includes theoretical writers such as Jameson (*The Prison-House of Language*), Lacan, Irigaray, Kristeva and Cixious; the inception and publication of journals such as *October, Heresies* and *m/f*, which appeared in 1976, 1977 and 1978 respectively; events as diverse as the fall of Saigon (1975) and the release of Poly-Styrene's single 'Oh Bondage up Yours' in 1977. The list reaches its teleological climax in 1978 with the publication of Judith Williamson's *Decoding Advertisements*.[2] The choice, I believe, is significant.

Subtitled 'Ideology and Meaning in Advertisements', Williamson's book correctly identifies the commodity not as a problem in economics but as the nucleus of a semantic crisis which is reticulated throughout the entire social system. Written in the scientific sounding vocabulary of semio-linguistics, Williamson's analysis appears starkly contrasted against the language of art history, with its deference for the ineffable and its privileging of the symbol as the paradigmatic model of meaning. Using the analytical 'tools' of semiology, structuralism, Freudian and post-Freudian psychoanalysis, Williamson claims that she would 'like to think of the title of the book as suggesting "dismantling cars" or something – a

sort of handbook'.[3] By providing a stable structure of interpretation to the
otherwise volatile flux of desire that advertising creates and exploits, semiology becomes, in her adept hands, a means of restoring meaning to those
areas of cultural life from which it may appear to have been lost.

The project Williamson engages with is that of demystification. Indeed
everything about the book speaks of this, from the austerity of the front
cover design, with its implication that this book needs no self-promotional
additives and that the potential readership needs no incitement to knowledge – glaringly contrasted against the cover of Cathy Myers' book,
Understains . . . the Sense and Seduction of Advertising,[4] with its emblazoned
if ironic announcement of 160 giant size pages – to the synoptic account of
intention on the back cover: 'It provides not an answer but a set of "tools"
which we can use to alter our perception of our society's subtlest and most
complex forms of propaganda.' What I would like to suggest is that Williamson's analysis, although never explicitly stated, of the 'real' affective
and propagandistic world of advertising imagery derives much of its force
from the posited existence of the 'image-inary' world of art production and
its attendant and 'ineffectual' academic discipline of art history. It is in this
negative sense, in which art is by implication established as an 'imaginary'
set up in order to rejuvenate in reverse the 'fiction of the real', that this
chapter attempts to examine the discourse of postmodernism and in particular the semiological refusal of the aesthetic. For it is a refusal that
conceals the possibility that traditional divisions have been recast in
scientific-sounding vocabulary. In the need to define the strategies that are
immanent in semiology's 'will to knowledge' it will be necessary to return
to its Lacanian 'other' – art history and art criticism.

In December 1986 the *Guardian* newspaper ran a three-part series
presenting various accounts of what it termed 'our post-modern malaise'
under the general heading the 'Crisis in Contemporary Culture'.[5] The
rhetorical tone of the series, as sampled by the header copy, was that of
fatalistic resignation. With the exception of Richard Gott's abbreviated
acknowledgement of the possibility of a 'progressive postmodernism' (*pace*
Hal Foster), the demise of modernism was universally lamented in terms
of the exhaustion of meaning. However, as fatigues go, the one reported by
the *Guardian* was far from pervasive. In fact many key modernist 'theoretical institutions' – pyschoanalysis, Marxism, structuralism and even art
history, the traditional punch-bag of methodological critique – escaped
unaffected. What emerged was a postmodernism of crisis and exhaustion
that was particular to art, or more accurately gained poignancy only in the
context of art. The 'art' of critique – the 'Difference' exhibition's attempt
to develop alternative and vital 'artistic' strategies and practices that no
longer looked to the worm-eaten props provided by the old-world support
systems of the gallery space and art historical legitimation – was ignored.

Instead the *Guardian* concentrated on the 'decadent' art that was being shown within these already declining institutions.

The crisis being reported was thus a phenomenological one. The epistemological ruptures and narrative breakdowns considered by many to predicate a postmodernity of instability, decadence and flux – the features isolated and highlighted in the *Guardian* articles – were notably absent. Art, it was reported, has merely contracted a temporary ailment, symbolised by the ascendancy of 'the media' and of media-related studies, and its own recourse to the dead forms of pastiche and parody. Reinforcing the old view of the visual arts as being in some way distinct from other spheres of culture (philosophy or, in this instance, postmodern theory), the *Guardian* therefore refused to articulate any account of postmodernity which problematised the nominalist distinctions between art, culture, meaning and language. Instead it presented us with an account of contemporary art that attempted to shoe-horn its phenomenological features into the sort of 'epistemic' categories that the new terminology of postmodernism fails to recognise. The result, in Gareth Stedman-Jones' words, is 'as if a Newtonian physicist were to come across Einstein, admit that relativity was a factor of some importance, and then attempt to carry on as before, under the impression that the occasional acknowledgement would absolve him from the necessity of further thought about it'.[6]

The scenario so far described is one in which the coherence of the concept art had in some miraculous way survived the onslaught and interrogations of what purported to be 'the crisis of contemporary culture'. This was most clearly evidenced by Waldemar Januszczak's contribution to the debate. According to him: 'Post-modernism has been distinguished by a lack of endemic subject matter, to go alongside a lack of educational and didactic and creative purpose.' (These we can only suppose are, for Januszczak, the distinguishing features of a modernist work.) He then goes on to describe the 'divine comedy' of postmodern artistic activity as 'a raggle-taggle protest movement with no obvious ambition for itself, no aesthetic consensus, involving a few successful artists and an awful lot of unsuccessful ones.'[7] At this point one is drawn into speculation regarding the criteria of success that underlie such a despotic pronouncement. Presumably they would be the very coherence, ambition and aesthetic consensus that confer authority on this type of connoisseurial criticism and that postmodern theory aims to problematise.

However, for all its heavy-handedness, Januszczak's contribution to the *Guardian* debate is *symptomatic* of a general unwillingness to treat 'art' as anything other than the reluctant victim of certain debased and unproductive theoretical discourses, whose appropriate field of activity lies elsewhere, in correspondingly debased areas of cultural activity. I am of course referring to 'the media' – and specifically popular culture as it appears on television and in advertising. The implication in his use of the metaphor of the historical pendulum is that, although it is to be recognised that contemporary art is indeed undergoing a period of crisis, the crisis is simply one of form, to be examined at a purely symptomatic level, and deplored, pending arts' reemergence in some less promiscuous and adulterated form. Interestingly enough, Judith Williamson's critique also operates primarily at this level of formal/structural analysis, ignoring what might be termed the crisis of aesthetics that has pervaded the commodity market as much as the art world. Both therefore contribute to the continued coherence of the two separate concepts – art and meaning – by maintaining them in opposition to one another. In other words, the 'crisis of meaning' is assumed to be a theoretical phenomenon, differentiated from an aesthetic crisis. It is a crisis that leaves the unitary concept 'art' unthreatened and unaffected. For both Williamson and Januszczak, whether conscious or not, the polarisation of semiology and aesthetics serves to maintain the cultural divisions upon which their respective institutional credibility is based. From this point of view, resistance to the poststructuralist collapse, or more accurately implosion, of meaning and aesthetics, can appear justified in terms of self-preservation alone.

Exclusions, lapses, silences ...

The contextualisation of this apparently antagonistic relationship between art and semiology requires a reconstruction of the concept of the sign that is so central to semiological analysis and indeed to the whole of the post-modern critique. This allows us to read backwards through the various theories that it was designed to replace. Most fundamentally it strikes at the archaic language theory that still informs a great deal of contemporary poetry and painting, namely the apprehension of language as names and meanings constituted as indissoluble links between words and things. Here I am reminded of the passage taken by Wittgenstein from St Augustine's *Confessions*:

> When they (my elders) named some object, and accordingly moved towards something, I saw this and I grasped that the thing was called by the sound they uttered when they meant to point it out. Their intention was shown by their bodily movements, as it were the natural language of all peoples: the expression of the face, the play of the eyes, the movement of other parts of the body, the tone of the voice which expresses our state of mind in seeking, having, rejecting, or avoiding something. Thus as I heard words repeatedly used in their proper places in various sentences, I gradually learnt to understand what objects they signified; and after I had trained my mouth to form these signs, I used them to express my own desires.[8]

Augustine's uncomplicated nominalist account of language is remarkably close to the writings of Ferdinand Saussure, the founding father of structuralist linguistics and of what has become the science of semiology. The two-sided nature of Saussure's sign, consisting as it does of a sound-image (signifier) and a concept (signified), means that the bond forged between any given signifier and signified appears arbitrary when viewed against the totality of possible relationships and combinations of the two elements (signifier and signified) that constitute the sign. Only when language and the operation of the sign are viewed synchronically, as part of a closed system where meaning is *fixed* in relation to the totality of other signs, does the unity that the sign imposes upon the two separate elements become comprehensible.

The material of semiology (the sign) and the task (the dissection of the sign in order 'scientifically' to establish or fix meaning) can be contrasted with art history, which takes as its subject the symbol; a unity that resists the semiological cleavage and separation. Instead we find that the symbol:

> fused together motion and stillness, turbulent content and organic form, mind and the world. Its material body was the medium of an absolute spiritual truth, one perceived by direct intuition rather than by any laborious process of critical analysis. In this sense the symbol brought such truths to bear on the mind which brooked no question: either you saw it or you didn't. It was the keystone of an irrationalism, a forestalling of reasoned critical inquiry, which has been rampant in critical theory ever since.[9]

The same sort of intuitional presupposition has dominated art history. Reinforced by the institutional apparatus of the museum, with its representation of history as the autonomous evolution of the creative spirit, and the art school, another bastion of liberal individualism, art history's preoccupation with the ineffability of symbolic truths has, as a policy of self-protection, made it particularly resistant to encroachments from those discourses associated with the theoretical positions of postmodernism. Deconstructive (semiotic) critical efforts seem, to the art historian, to be more appropriately directed towards those areas of culture that are self-consciously constructed as systems of value creation – for instance, advertising, in which desire becomes a function of the sign – rather than the questioning of the disciplinary boundaries that allow such distinctions to be made in the first place. Given the genealogy of art history as a discipline, embedded as it has been in reactionary politics, connoisseurial prejudice and the conservation of artefacts and values, this comes as no surprise. But the fact that the two modes of analysis have remained separate seems to suggest something else. The mutual exclusions serving to separate and distinguish the two discourses are rooted in the same will to survive: a will which necessitates the maintenance, overtly or tacitly, of a unitary concept of art as the sole domain of the aesthetic.

What seems to be called for, if this is indeed the case, is a 'psychoan-alytical' critique of the overt discourse of semiology of the sort that Foucault performs with sexuality.[10] As with sexuality, the strategies of power that are immanent in the particular will to knowledge of semiology are directly related to its ability to hide its own mechanisms. The semi-ological injunction to silence over the issue of art and aesthetic production is by implication a claim that there is nothing to see or know from such things. In the introductory part of *The History of Sexuality* (vol. 1) of the repressive hypothesis, Foucault had this to say about the silences of dis-course:

> Silence itself – the thing that one declines to say, or is forbidden to name, the discretion that is required between different speakers – is less the absolute limit of discourse, the other side from which it is separated by a strict boundary, than an element that functions alongside the things said, with them and in relation to them within overall strategies. There is no binary division made between what one says and what one does not say; we must try and determine the different ways of not saying things, how those who can and those who cannot speak of them are distributed, which type of discourse is authorised, or which form of discretion is required in either case. There is not one but many silences, and they are an integral part of the strategies that underlie and permeate discourses.[11]

This passage gains a particular resonance when seen against the resolute binarism that divides and separates media semiology from critical pro-nouncements regarding the state of contemporary 'postmodern' art pro-duction. Any attempt to clarify this situation must take into consideration the absences, deferrals and silences that Foucault points us towards. The particular way in which semiology interrogates the production of meaning in imagery must therefore be examined through the analysis not only of the type of question that it asks but also from the point of view of those questions that it cannot ask and those issues that it refuses to address.

Turning away from the traditional analytical procedure that seeks essence at the centre or focal point of a particular discourse, we must now seek out the contours of the problematic which, in determining what it includes within its field, also and necessarily determines what is excluded from it. The concepts that are excluded (absences, lacunae), and the prob-lems that are not posed adequately (semi-silences, lapses), or not posed at all (silences), are therefore as much a part of the problematic as are the concepts and problems that are present. This sub-discourse of silences, lapses and absences, because it escapes the context of the continuous incitement to discourse and truth under which the real mechanisms of misunderstanding operate, resists interrogation from the model that has administered its silence. It also defines the scope and outer limits of the discourse or model in question. Put another way, what is being said is that the model, in this case the semiological model, can question every level of coherence except its own, since all discourses function simultaneously as both the instrument and the effect of power. With this in mind we see that information returned from the process of interrogation or questioning – in this instance, the functioning of the sign within the syntagmatic enclosure of meaning – is always as the question imagines and solicits it to be. The question assimilates the answer, absorbing or regurgitating it in decodable form or inventing and anticipating it in predictable form.

Baudrillard invokes a similar paradox when he quotes from Michael Tort's book *Intelligence Quotient*:

> What is going to determine the answer to the question is not just the question as such in the form in which it was posed, it is also the idea that the subject forms about the most appropriate tactic to adopt in function of the concept he has formed about the expectations of the inter-rogator.[12]

The subject, in this case the media, is thus preconstituted by the type of questions that are asked – questions which themselves are determined in part by predicted interrogational responses. To escape this Moebian circularity, if only temporarily, what seems to be required is a symptomatic reading of semiology whereby the explicit discourse is read conjointly with the absences, lacunae and silences which, constituting a second 'silent' discourse, are so many symptoms of the 'unconscious' problematic buried in its explicit practice.

What needs to be shown is that exactly the same procedure of exclusion that had protected the disciplinary definition of art history seems to be taking place in reverse, from the opposite deconstructive camp. (We shall return to this question later by re-examining the relationship between aesthetics and meaning.) Whereas art history had been a minority disci-pline, in that it was continually threatened by the encroachments of popu-lar culture, the currently dominant postmodern mode of analysis, which ostensibly at least refuses the high/low culture dichotomy, appears to be colluding in the preservation of the category 'art' by failing to address it at all. This is most clearly evidenced by Marshall Blonsky's anthology, *On Signs*,[13] which has assumed a position as a seminal postmodern text, and in which semio-linguistic analysis is applied to areas of culture that range from the Royal Wedding as mediatised spectacle, to the 'Love-life of the Hippopotamus'. However, of the 44 texts included, from a list of authors that reads like a hagiography of postmodern intelligentsia (Eco, Barthes, Lacan, Kristeva, Derrida, Foucault, Jameson and, as it proudly an-nounces on the front cover, 'many others'), not a single text even indirectly addresses the issue of art as it has been traditionally defined.

A number of possible conclusions might be drawn from this. For, granted that art does take part in the matrix of sign production and exchange that constitutes our culture, there must, one supposes, be some rationale behind its exclusion from an analysis of that culture. It could be, for instance, that the Saussurian model for the analysis of signs in some way proves inadequate when dealing with those signs that are produced within the context of art. Alternatively, and somewhat more persuasively, we could suspect postmodern cultural analysis of a submerged desire to protect art in its separation from other spheres of culture. Is it perhaps a sublimated or at least unacknowledged desire to retain an area of aesthetic purity uncontaminated by the pervasive pollution of popular culture, which, although celebrated in the attentiveness and rigour of its analysis, is covertly despised in form? Like art history, it might be that semiological deconstruction is not impartial.

Art: A genealogy of the term

The permeation of the aesthetic into every aspect of postmodern cultural life – leisure (Eco), the presentation of the self (Hebdige), commodities (Haug), ethics (Rorty) and even 'reality' (Baudrillard) – although it has a discernible history running from Baudelaire's nineteenth-century vision of the dandy through to Warhol's celebrations of everyday banalities, cannot be made comprehensible unless juxtaposed to the modernist or formalist account of the aesthetic against which it is thown into relief. So before we turn to the postmodern 'explosion' of the aesthetic, we must examine the conditions of its containment within the arts under the modernist regime.

Exploring this position further necessitates a re-examination of the modernist notion of self-development which, following Habermas, proceeds according to its own 'internal logic'.[14] Although it is only a partial account of modernism within the arts, the formalist aesthetic provides the most explicit statement of this development. It was the notion of 'ostranae', or defamiliarisation, the distancing of objects from any straight-forward existential contact, that Schlovsky and subsequent formalists were to isolate as the moment of aestheticisation. The formalist model that emerged was based on the notion of defamiliarisation, a notion which is further complicated by the necessary inclusion of the hypothesis of per-petual change; an hypothesis which involves a complicated system of mutations and adjustments. The familiar, the existentially available, is thus, according to the formalist aesthetic, denied by the practice of the 'bearing of the device'. (A similar process could be taking place within the field of commodities when the commodity relinquishes the signified seen as use value, and presents itself in terms of the signifier alone and its endless commutability, as an index of exchange. Interestingly enough, it is this moment – when the commodity becomes a sort of 'pure object' – that Baudrillard identifies as the point at which the commodity becomes aes-theticised.) In this sense modernist art and literature, which defamiliarises its own techniques, is to be radically distinguished from the older art and literature in which the devices are deliberately concealed. (Hence, it is the so-called 'self-consciousness' of Manet that is often taken by art historians to indicate the birth of modernism within the visual arts.)

Obviously if the notion of defamiliarisation is to be taken seriously as an aesthetic principle, it must posit some grounding notion of the familiar or real, from which it can be distinguished. However, if the real itself is produced, existing solely in representation, or at least is continually thrown into crisis and doubt, the formalist principle of defamiliarisation, if not unworkable, certainly takes on a wholly new set of implications. The same doubts translate to the specific concerns of the (formalist) artists. Since if the 'bearing of the device' is indeed one of the distinguishing characteristics of specifically modern art, it also seems to be characteristic of all artistic production (though not all artistic appropriation – e.g. primitive artefacts) so long as the term art is to retain any degree of autonomy and to distinguish itself from rather than dissolve into other areas of 'life'.

According to this formulation, all artistic and literary structures may be understood as taking themselves as their own object, in other words, as being primarily about art or literature themselves. Thus the specific and unique structure of (formalist) modernism in the artistic/literary sphere turns out to be no more than the basic structure of art and literature in general. This paradox can be expressed in another way. Defamiliarisation must always be polemical and dependent on the negation of existing habits of thought and perception. The concept therefore is not a coherent one in its own right but one that is transitional and self-abolishing. In Jameson's words,

> the 'tragic sense of life' implicit in the formalist idea of perpetual change, demands a kind of consent to change and to the inevitable wearing out of once new procedures, in short to one's own death . . . yet the 'bearing of the device' is not just one technique amongst others, but rather the coming to consciousness of art as defamiliarisation in the first place. So if it goes, the entire theory goes with it and what gave itself as a universal law proves with the turning of the calendar to have been nothing more than the ideology of the day in disguise.[15]

If the concept art is indeed nothing more than the ideology of the day in disguise, then its continued survival, within an environment that ostensibly militates against its very existence, must be examined within the terms of an ideology of postmodern theory. Ideology after all does not exist in some place apart, as the discourse of the dominant class before being channelled through the media. Just as art commodities cannot be shown to possess any ontological status independent of the form that they take in the operation of the exchange system, so the ideology of theory is not some 'imaginary' floating in the wake of exchange value, but rather the very operation of exchange itself, with the exclusions, absences, lapses and displacements that such an exchange entails. Thus it becomes apparent that the linguistic or conceptual coherence of the identifiable entity art must itself be dependent upon exactly the sort of exclusions and absences that constitute the ideological process.

A convincing and useful account of this process, approaching the problematic from a different angle, is provided by Roger Taylor in 'The Marxist Theory of Art'.[16] Taylor, wishing to retain the 'open concept' theory of art as the only possible anti-essentialist account of it, maintains that it is only minimally explanatory unless the detailing of the open concept involves a social perspective. The social perspective that Taylor chooses to examine is the evaluative nature of art as a subcategory of one of the four attitudes identified by the social scientist Iwansha as constituting the four basic orientations towards our environment; cognitive, moral, activist and aesthetic.[17] As Taylor points out (and here I have to reduce a subtle and complex argument to the level of assertion): 'To say that a novel is a work of art is, within a standard setting, to evaluate it favorably compared to other novels from which this categorisation is withheld.'[18] Art is now constituted as a subcategory of the more general categories of music, painting, sculpture, etc., in that it is set up as the range of notably superior instances within that category. This distinction involves a stress on valuation that aesthetic theory as much as semiology has been unwilling to effect. As an example of this, Taylor directs the reader towards Richard Wollheim's disclaimer at the end of *Art and Its Objects* as typifying this sort of aesthetic evasion: 'It will be observed that in this essay next to nothing has been said about the subject that dominates contemporary aesthetics, that is the evaluation of art and its logical character. This omission is deliberate.'[19] And finally we arrive at the edge of a possible link between contemporary art practice, semiology and postmodernism. For within the context of advertising and semiology, rather than art and aesthetics, Judith Williamson makes a similar omission. We might reasonably suspect it of being equally deliberate.

Perhaps part of the reluctance of cultural commentators to acknowledge the intrusion of value as being central to our notion of art as a subcategory, is that it implies a bonding process that links 'art' with all its transcendent connotations to the often ugly specifics of our particular phase within the development of late capitalism. This is because the concept of value cannot be understood abstractly but must be interpreted socially, as an instrument of social difference. The nature of this linking has been usefully summarised by J. Adkins Richardson:

The appearance of art as distinct from craft or skill is a phenomenon of modern history. Raymond Williams, in *Culture and Society*, shows that this use of the term comes into common English during the last decades of the eighteenth century in company with the use of 'culture' to designate the norm opposed to that of the despised masses.

Only as capital and industry make possible the total democratisation of life is there any serious demand from the highly literate for prescriptions of eliteness to distinguish their values from those of the common folk. It can be argued to considerable effect that the very notion of absolute standards of decorum in life was already a response to the incursions of the 'patent nobility' (drawn from the wealthy middle class) upon the ancient privileges of the nobility of gentle birth.[20]

Richardson goes on to point out that the notion of exclusive value has a discernible history, first appearing as an invention of the aristocracy and used as a means of distinguishing the superiority of its form of life to that of the revolutionary bourgeoisie. Subsequently the victorious bourgeoisie took over the concept in part out of their aspirations to be the ruling class. Crudely outlined, we begin to develop an analytical schema in which changes in the concept of art can be correlated and determined by changes in the development of capital.

So if we are to accept Taylor's convincingly argued claim that 'the category art which we possess is no older than capitalism itself',[21] then any discussion regarding the status of the category art (in this instance in its relationship to semiology) must take into account the phase in the development of capitalism corresponding to the moment of analysis. Furthermore, if we are to accept that our present era is in some way post-capitalist or neo-capitalist, in the sense that we are no longer dominated by capital in the straightforward Marxian sense but by the power and commutability of the signifier circulating with a fatal conformity to the code, then the category 'art' must also be reevaluated within this new and recently changed context. It is a category which, as I have argued, has been persistently exempted from the semiological critique – a curious omission when viewed against the postmodern (postcapitalist) tendency to find *all* meanings, let alone 'aesthetics', within the play and exchange of signs. The plot thickens (rather than deepens) as the category of art emerges as a silent discourse that the semiological method refuses to enunciate. But here what is at stake is not the methodology but the intentions of those who apply it – who seem to wish to reconstitute the category art as a media – transcendent 'imaginary' that escapes the cruel order imposed by the code and provides a metaphysical corrective for the debased and fascinated aesthetic of the hyperreal.

Aestheticising the real

According to Jean Baudrillard, it is the continual transmutation of the real into the hyperreal that is the distinguishing feature of our present phase of capitalism. It is a phase that is no longer controlled by the circulation of exchange value in the immediate form of capital. Instead it is the shadow of exchange, the 'genetic code' of the media that has come to determine rather than merely represent the ebbs and flows of capital and the structuring of the capitalist economy. This is the point at which simulation displaces the principle of reproduction and becomes the reigning scheme of our current phase – dominated no longer by capital but by the code and its structural law of value. Simulation, defined as the creation of copies for which there are no originals, effaces the distinction between the 'produced' symptom and the real symptom, the shadow and the substance, the imaginary and the real. Representation is now no more than an issue of equivalence as sign and reality implode into one another. In a familiar passage from 'Simulations', Baudrillard attacks the dualities of reality and representation, truth and falsity upon which the project of modernity has rested; 'The very definition of the real has become that which it is possible to give an equivalent representation . . . the real is not only that which can be reproduced, but that which is already reproduced, the hyperreal which is entirely simulation.'[22]

Hyperreality can be seen, following Baudrillard, as the circuiting of codes rather than meaning within the system of symbolic exchange; the absolute form of the code circulating free of its referent, its objective reality or material alibi. In such self-regulating systems the signifier becomes its own referent in tautological repetition of itself. Baudrillard writes that the era of simulation

> begins with the commutability of terms that were once contradictory or dialectically opposed . . . In politics of the left and the right, in the media of true and false, in objects of utility and uselessness, and of nature and culture on the very level of signification. All the great humanist criteria have been effaced in our system of images and signs. Everything has become undecided – this is the characteristic effect of domination by the code which rests on the principle of neutralisation and indifference.[23]

Reflexivity, traditionally the critical component of self-consciousness and self-scrutiny, has lost its critical force in the era of simulation. Exacerbated to the extremes of corrosive uncertainty, the reflexive impulse has become one of pure implosion collapsing all polarities into the black hole of simulated indifference. What we accept as reality, with all its depth, texture and perspicacity, now appears as no more than a fabrication of effects, a 'tactical hallucination' designed to stand in for reality's absence and act out the immolation of our desire.

The shift described by Baudrillard from an era dominated by the principles and logos of (re)production to that of simulation is one that is reticulated most evidently within the systems of meaning that are the subject of semiological analysis. Forms can no longer be said to change at the moment of reproduction – the moment analysed by Williamson – but rather as soon as they are conceived from the point of view of their reproducibility as diffracted from the generating nucleus of the model. With this implosion of meaning we are denied the old-fashioned luxury of the morally self-righteous ideological critique. For

> once short-circuited, the myths (the only danger capital confronted historically came from the mythical exigency of rationality that accompanied it from the beginning) in an operationality of fact without discourse, once capital has become its own myth, or rather an interminable machine, aleatory, something like a social genetic code, it no longer leaves any room for planned reversal; and this is its true violence.[24]

With the neutralisation of the signified by the code, the entire system of communication passes from that of being syntactically complex (the closed system analysed by Saussure) to a binary system of question and answer. Every message becomes a verdict, the simulacrum of distance or even of contradiction between the two poles becoming only like the effect of the real that the sign seems to emit, a 'tactical hallucination'. It is a binary schema of question and answer which, whilst maintaining the illusion of choice, renders inarticulate every discourse. This interrogational relexivity confounds every attempt to restore the meaning process. For instance, in our analysis of the media, or more specifically Williamson's analysis of advertising, the techniques of montage and codification demand that we construe and decode by observing the same procedure used when the work was assembled. The reading of the message then becomes simply the perpetual examination of the code. Like the fox chasing its own tail, simulation appears to be constantly reaching beyond itself. But the appearance is itself a simulacrum, for as we learn from Baudrillard: 'Whereas representation tries to absorb simulation by interpreting it as false representation, simulation envelops the whole edifice of representation as itself a simulacrum.'[25]

So within the orbital recurrence of models and the simulated generation of difference we are denied the possibility of maintaining determinate positions of power and discourse. The ideological analysis of meaning which is the cornerstone of the semiological project, in its attempts to restore the objective process, is still involved in a theology of truth and secrecy to which the notion of ideology continues to belong. However, as Baudrillard makes clear: 'It is no longer a question of a false representation of reality but of concealing the fact that the real is no longer real and thus of saving the reality principle.'[26] An analysis of the sort performed by Williamson, in its determination to elucidate different layers of meaning, engages with the reality principle at the level of reconstruction. However, in the police-like order of the lucid described by Baudrillard, in which the simulacra hide nothing as they have nothing to conceal, meaning has already given way to fascination; a fascination demanded by a discourse of empty surfaces in which the stability of correspondences which gave the sign system meaning has imploded, leaving only a colloidal flux.

Within this flux the sign no longer functions according to the despotic relationship between signifier and signified that is the key to structural semiology. Evidence of this type of breakdown can easily be found in 'Music Television' (MTV) which in its self-conscious abandonment of the reality principle and submission to the simulacrum becomes a metaphor for the postmodern condition itself. In MTV the original, the copy, the same, and the like are displaced by simulacra that no longer bear the nostalgia of creativity. Its implosive ambience and hypervisibility conceal nothing, and in the process MTV call semiotics into question: it has no space or scene of operation. In effect, it 'sidesteps the mediation of reason'. The semiological 'logic and difference, of distinction' cannot explain MTV's ecstatic intensity: semiotics moves 'too slow'.[27] When reality becomes merely an effect of the sign, and the logos that was implied by the coupling of the signifier and the signified breaks down, so meaning gives way to fascination.

If, as in MTV, signs now concatenate and produce themselves without any basic reference to sustain them, semiology can appear only as an attempt to save meaning at precisely the point at which it was already lost – in other words it becomes a nostalgic project aiming to produce meaning through the 'domestication' of the sign. The differences between the mode of attention demanded by the aesthetic object and the commodity that *had* sustained the semiological preoccupation with meaning can now no longer be observed. As a result the attendant disciplines of aesthetics and semiology are forced into an uneasy but mutual alliance as neither can do more than maintain the appearance of difference in a nostalgic attempt to recreate their lost objects. Neither meaning nor art escapes the omnipresent banality of the simulacrum. In Baudrillard's vision of postmodernity we find that

> art is everywhere, since artifice is at the very heart of reality. And so art is dead, not because its critical transcendence has gone, but because reality itself, entirely impregnated by an aesthetic which is inseparable from its own structure, has become confused with its own image.[28]

In this passage Baudrillard offers a route to understanding why art, which apparently was suffocated by the undifferentiated fields of media semiurgy, should have been resurrected by the very discourse that supposedly signalled its end. The difference component, the 'other' of identity has, in both practice and discourse, virtually disappeared, as reality itself loses its own guarantor, its representational other, and becomes art/ificial. It is an artificiality that threatens semiology as much as art criticism/history. In looking at the unconscious or latent discourse of semiology, the aim has been to reveal that the necessary conditions of its survival are in fact very similar to those of its apparently adversarial discipline, art history.

With this thesis in mind, Judith Williamson simply becomes a latter-day Kenneth Clarke. Both vigorously defend against the omnipresent and impartial encroachments of simulation. Both disciplines need to demarcate the aesthetic, to protect it from the (non)aesthetic of fascination, in other words to preserve the concept 'art' as a coherent entity. With semiology this entity becomes a component of difference, an 'imaginary' that functions to maintain the important distinctions between meaning, value and aesthetics on which the validity of the semiological project rests.

By concentrating on meaning alone, the discourse of semiology reinvests in the concept of art as the sole domain of the aesthetic, thus significantly avoiding the problem posed by a postmodern aesthetic that has permeated every aspect of social existence – the process described by Baudrillard. In this way the continued existence of art as a coherent concept not only serves to protect the semiological discourse from the difficult problematic posed by the aesthetic and the assignation of value that Taylor has shown to be part of that process, but also from the total disintegration of the very notion of meaning in the face of the aesthetics of fascination. The semiological inability to deal with this aesthetic is paradoxically – when one thinks that its concentration on meaning was in part a response to art history's preoccupation with value – due to its reliance on the preservation of the value-determined subcategory of art. However, the 'imaginary' art that we find silently resurrected, as part of the validation process described earlier, is not that of art as a critical entity that can contest the media or ironically collude with it, but rather as a nostalgic referent. As a compensating device for the loss of the real, the nostalgic referent art constitutes a stable entity against which the preoccupation with meaning alone begins to look pertinent. However, the victory of semiology is a phyrric one that witnesses the evanescence of the object at the moment of its capture and stabilisation. Baudrillard himself, writing in a different context, about ethnology, described a similar process when he remarked that 'For ethnology to live its object must die. But the latter revenges itself for dying by having been discovered, and defies by its death the science that wants to take hold of it.'[29] Thus, in a perverse way art is indebted to semiology for still being art, in that it has become 'what it used to be', that which semiotics in its absences has made it – simulacra art, which proclaims only the universal truth of semiology.

Notes

1 Published in the 'Difference' exhibition catalogue, 1985.
2 Judith Williamson, *Decoding Advertisements* (Boyars, 1978).
3 Ibid., p. 9.
4 Cathy Myers, *Understains* (Comedia, 1986).
5 *Guardian*, 1/2 December 1986.

6 Gareth Stedman-Jones, 'History: the Poverty of Empiricism', in Blackburn (ed.) *Ideology in Social Science* (Fontana, 1972).

7 Waldemar Januszczak, *Guardian*, 2 Dec 1986.

8 See Wittgenstein, *Philosophical Investigations* (Blackwell, 1958) 1:1.

9 Terry Eagleton, *Literary Theory* (Blackwell, 1983) p.22.

10 Michel Foucault, *The History of Sexuality*, vol. 1 (Penguin, 1984).

11 Ibid., p.27.

12 Quoted in Jean Baudrillard, 'Simulations', (Semiotext(e), 1983), p. 123.

13 Marshall Blonsky (ed.), *On Signs* (Blackwell, 1985).

14 See Habermas, 'Modernity – An Incomplete Project' in Hal Foster (ed.) *Postmodern Culture* (Pluto, 1985).

15 Frederic Jameson, *The Prison-house of Language; A Critical Account of Structuralism and Russian Formalism* (Princeton University Press, 1972) p.90.

16 Roger Taylor, 'The Marxist Theory of Art', *Radical Philosophy*, vol.3.

17 Iwansha, 'Without Art', *British Journal of Aesthetics*, Oct 1971.

18 Roger Taylor, 'Marxist Theory of Art', p.32.

19 Richard Wollheim, *Art and its Objects* (N.Y., 1968).

20 J. Adkins Richardson, 'Illustration and Art', *British Journal of Aesthetics*, Oct 1971.

21 Roger Taylor, 'Marxist Theory of Art', p.33.

22 Jean Baudrillard, 'Simulations', p. 146.

23 Ibid., p.12.

24 Ibid., p. 112.

25 Ibid., p.11.

26 Ibid., p.25.

27 See Baudrillard, 'The Child in The Bubble', *Impulse*, 11 (4), 1985, p.13.

28 Baudrillard, 'Simulations', pp. 151–2.

29 Ibid., p.13.

4 The Cultural Logic of Nostalgia

When the real is no longer what it used to be, nostalgia assumes its full meaning. There is a proliferation of myths of origin and signs of reality; of second-hand truth, objectivity and authenticity. There is an escalation of the true, of the lived experience; a resurrection of the figurative where the object and substance have disappeared. And there is a panic-stricken production of the real and the referential, above and parallel to the panic of material production: this is how simulation appears in the phase that concerns us – a strategy of the real, neo-real and hyperreal whose universal double is a strategy of deterrence.

Jean Baudrillard, *Simulations*

Elusive depth models

In what has been described by Baudrillard as the 'spiralling Moebian compulsion' of the postmodern discourse, Frederic Jameson's article, 'The Cultural Logic of Late Capitalism'[1] has assumed a position of seminality, in part, I suspect because of its level-headedness. Resisting the hyperbole and inflamed denunciations that had hitherto characterised theoretical commentaries of postmodernism, Jameson takes a wholesomely traditional 'leftist' approach, attempting to periodise postmodernism in relation to the economic systems of late capital. Adopting the term 'late capitalism' from Ernest Mandel[2] – Mandel distinguishes three stages of capitalism: market capitalism; monopoly capitalism; and *Spatkapitalismus* – multinational, 'late' capitalism – Jameson, who regards it as 'the purest form of capital yet to have emerged'[3], uses it to describe a hegemonic norm or dominant cultural logic against which the morphology of postmodernism can be determined. Although never described or developed, the reader is expected, in an act of suspended disbelief, to maintain some conception of this abstract norm as a means of resisting the view of present history as 'sheer heterogeneity, random difference, a coexistence of a host of distinct forces whose effectivity is undecidable'.[4] Against this conceptual ambiguity the analysis appears to invoke no moral judgement. With its shirt-sleeve and 'perfectly faded denim' approach, Jameson escorts us through the various constitutive features of postmodernism – The Rise of Aesthetic Populism ... The Waning of

Affect ... The Fate of Real History ... The Abolition of Critical Distance ... etc. – concepts and commentary viewed and heard as if through the tinted windows of a tourbus visiting unfamiliar territories in order to reinscribe the familiarity of those that have been left behind – the 'imaginary' set up in order to rejuvenate in reverse the fiction of the real. The nature of this 'reality', for Jameson, is to be found in the so-called hegemonic norm or dominant cultural logic that seems to be so resistant to either analysis or description.

The fatigue and senility of modernism in the 1980s can, according to Jameson, be directly associated with two concurrent tendencies that have progressively eroded the modernist dynamic. One such impulse might be found in the canonisation of the great modernist works of 'resistance', the acculturation of the anti-cultural and the institutionalisation of the subversive. The other is to be found in what he terms a 'rise in aesthetic populism', a tendency epitomised by Robert Venturi's *Learning from Las Vegas*. In drawing attention to the effacement of the distinction between high culture and mass or commercial culture Venturi begins to describe the postmodern fascination for the degraded aesthetic landscape of schlock, kitsch and the TV serial. It is a form of consumer eclecticism that is the by-product of wholesale and rampant commodification, and which has been described in less celebratory terms by Lyotard as, 'the degree zero of contemporary culture; one listens to reggae, watches a Western, eats Macdonald's food for lunch and local cuisine for dinner, wears Paris perfume in Tokyo and "retro" clothes in Hong Kong'. Knowledge, according to Lyotard, has become 'a matter of T.V. games'.[5] It is an aesthetic of eclectic populism whose only common denominator is the process of commodification. Under such a regime of pervasive, almost viral commodification, everything from cuisine to sentiment finds its reality in the chameleon surfaces of the image – in its acquisition and exchange. The once trustworthy world of appearances has now been replaced by an infinitely mutable set of texts or simulacra.

For Jameson, the most important effect of the transition towards the kind of postmodern culture that he describes is the loss of credibility in the 'depth model' that had until recently premissed our cultural self-understanding. These are the models upon which the modernist project rested – the dialectical model of essential and apparent, the Freudian model of latent and manifest, the existential model of authentic and inauthentic, the semiotic model of signifier and signified, etc. – and which provide an episteme that presupposes the value of hermeneutics and the heuristic approach to knowledge. Meaning, where it has appeared to be absent, indeterminate or inaccessible, has in fact merely been latent, waiting to be revealed by successive acts of excavation and penetration. The dialectics of essence and appearance and inside and outside encourage a distrust of surface and the sort of analysis that seeks to peel off dissimulating superficialities in order to reveal an underlying reality and truth that somehow exists apart from and beyond the immediate object of analysis. As an interpretive model, the depth model therefore works only on the vertical axis. It is this operationality that postmodernism contests.

To illustrate the difference between the modern depth analysis and the postmodern discourse of surface, Jameson compares Van Gogh's 'Peasant Shoes', with Andy Warhol's 'Diamond Dust Shoes'. Taking Van Gogh's 'Peasant Shoes', he claims that if, after copious reproduction, the image is not to sink to the level of mere decoration it is necessary to reconstruct the initial situation out of which the work emerges. This is done via the hermeneutical reading suggested by Heidegger in *Der Ursprung des Kunstwerkes*. In its inert objectual form, the work is seen to acquire significance only as a symptom of the vaster reality that replaces it as its ultimate truth – in this case the truth and reality of peasant toil, drudgery and hardship – or, as Dan Latimer puts it, the truth of the activity of art in general 'as the mediating entity between the wordless chthonic powers of Nature and the civilised realm of the human and the historical that Heidegger calls the "world".'[6] Contrasting with this is the work by Warhol which resists the acquisition of significance in its celebration of the hallucinogenic intensity of a depthless surface. The literal superficiality of Warhol's shoes (the surface twinkles with gilt sand), bereft as they are of history or use, places them within a cycle of circulation that no longer lays claim to any particular truth bar that of its own reproducibility.

What is revealing about Jameson's analysis is that he acknowledges that it can only be through the mental reconstruction (or more appropriately projection) of a vanished past that Van Gogh's 'Peasant Shoes' can escape becoming 'an inert object' or 'reified end-product ... unable to be grasped as a symbolic act in its own right',[7] the clearly lamentable fate of Warhol's footwear. The implication that meaning resides in the reconstructive apparatus that privileges a particular reading of the work – in this case the hermeneutical reading – is telling. For such a reading is offered, as Jameson acknowledges, in part, as a compensatory device for the progressive effacement of meaning via the popularisation of the image through its reproduction – as a way of saving the image from becoming 'mere decoration'. But here we must question Jameson's motives. Does the depth model, in salvaging the work from the aesthetic junkyard of the present, provide an exclusive or merely a preferred reading of the 'Peasant Shoes'? And has not the anguish of the original creative investment been all but effaced as the image becomes a new kitschy divinity that can now merrily coexist with triplets of ducks climbing flock wallpaper? What emerges out of the comparison of the two sets of shoes is a view of postmodernism that regards it not as a cultural dominant – a pervasive mode of consumption – but rather as a mode of cultural production, characterised by its celebration of blankness, depthlessness and indifference, and apotheosised in Andy Warhol. Constituting postmodernism in this way allows Jameson to indulge in a nostalgia for a paradise lost of stable meanings and fixed coordinates of value. Were a reproduction of Jameson's own shoes to be introduced into the debate at this point, one might reasonably expect them to be, once taken out of the glossy postmodern box, of the old fashioned hermeneutical variety.

Expression and interpretation

Nostalgia, as eloquently stated by Baudrillard, comes into play as a compensatory device when the reality principle appears to be under threat. The principle under contestation throughout 'The Cultural Logic of Late Capitalism' is that of authenticity. Jameson's rejection of postmodernism, and by implication popular culture, is on the grounds that both are tainted with commodification and therefore 'inauthentic'. To illustrate the point another comparison is made; this time between Warhol's 'Marilyn', and Munch's 'Scream'. Both images have a history of considerable reproduction – the work by Munch was originally circulated in lithographic form. Both images are thought to be representative of, or to embody, a particular era or zeitgeist. For Jameson, Munch's 'Scream' has become the 'canonical expression of the great modernist thematics of alienation, anomie, solitude and social fragmentation and isolation, a virtually programmatic emblem of what used to be called the age of anxiety'.[8] It presupposes a separation within the subject, a metaphysics of inside and outside, and can be understood as the cathartic externalisation of an internal emotion. In contrast, Warhol's 'Marilyn' offers no metaphysical reading and discards the depth model of inside and outside. The representation is of a star who has become commodified to the extent of being indecipherable from her own image. Again Guy Debord's phrase comes to mind. She is the perfect representative of a society in which the image has 'become the final form of commodity reification . . . the spectacle is capital to such a degree that it becomes the image.'[9]

The very concept of expression is therefore seen to presuppose a separation within the subject. Far from being trans-historical, such separation is shown to be specific to the ideology of modernism. From his analysis of the 'Scream', Jameson goes on to argue that there is a sort of historicism to concepts such as anxiety and alienation that has become discernible only recently. (The current vogue for 'neo-expressionist' painting illustrates this point – 'expression' is now commodified and marketed under the sign of the 'neo'. Originally 'authentic' emotions are recycled within the art market as an inherited set of styles or postures.) The historicism of modernism is now seen to engender a correspondingly historicist account of subjectivity. The great Warhol figures, Marilyn, Edie Sedgewick, Charles Manson, etc., with their experiential proximity to drugs and schizophrenia, are contrasted with the hysterics and neurotics analysed by Freud, whose experiences can be characterised only within the idiolect of modernism: in terms of solitude, private revolt, Van Gogh-type madness and so on. (Of course the boundaries that separate such characterisations of experience are never static – one might think of a recent attempt by Judy and Fred Vermorel to realign a Freudian based notion of hysteria within the specifically postmodern consumer context of teenage pop-idolisation.[10]) The concept of the alienated subject of modernism has thus been lost as subjectivity has been fragmented and dispersed across the much wider psychological force-field of postmodernism.

If, as Jameson maintains, the problem of expression is inextricably linked to a notion of the subject as monad-like container, then the end of the bourgeois ego/monad heralds the end not only of the psychopathologies of that ego but also the creative projections that were both its expression and its form. Exit the storm-tossed monad of bourgeois individualism, the alienated outsider, angst-ridden and nauseated by contingency, fear and trembling. However, with him/her also goes the conception of a unique style, which had been dependent on the preservation of the notion of the centred subject, and is increasingly jeopardised as the centring power of the ego comes under threat. Although for some (*pace* Deleuze and Guattari) this threat to the supposed unity of the bourgeois ego is redeployed to provide the basis for a radically new conceptualisation of experience, for Jameson it is described only in terms of loss – in particular, the loss of the notion of style as being individual, inimitable and therefore authentic. In his own words, postmodernism means the end of 'style, in the sense of the unique and personal, the end of the distinctive individual brushstroke which results in the collapse of the high modernist ideology of style – what is as unique and unmistakable as your own fingerprints, as incomparable as your own body'. [11]

It is significant that the body should be chosen as the site of struggle in the contestation of identity and therefore the category of 'personal expression'. One has only to think of the existential/romantic critical rhetoric surrounding the work of an artist such as Pollock to periodise Jameson's nostalgic pinings. The 'trace' of the expressive gesture or body, the actual use of the fingerprint, the painting as psychological seismograph all acted as terms that reinscribed the romantic view of the artist as mediator in the struggle between internalised emotion/creativity and external form, the view of the artist as alienated but enlightened outsider. Contextualising the artist in these terms might begin to suggest that the cultural dominant or 'hegemonic norm' against which Jameson's analysis takes place is not in fact the credible (within the quasi-Marxist terms established) category of late or multinational capitalism but rather that of high-modernism, which, as the analysis proceeds, becomes increasingly confused with high-romanticism.

Deprived of the centring capacity of the unified and unifying self, modernist styles quickly become postmodern codes, in a field of stylistic and discursive 'heterogeneity without norm'. This problematises not just the availability of the older category of 'personal expression' in terms of cultural production, but also the way in which the consuming subject would respond. According to Jameson, the loss of centred self that had premissed the modernist notion of 'personal expression' has also entailed the loss of a subject capable of articulating or experiencing any feeling at all. It is then claimed that 'This is not to say that the cultural products of the postmodern era are utterly devoid of feeling, but rather that such feelings – which it may be better and more accurate to call "intensities" – are now free-floating and impersonal, and tend to be dominated by a peculiar kind of euphoria'.[12] In a subsequent interview Lyotard claimed that the feelings in question 'have nothing to do with feelings that offer clues to meaning in the way anxiety did'.[13] Are they then momentary feelings – feelings that have no permanence and are quickly overlaid by successive events, like phosphorescence sparkling in the wake of the signifiers of emotion? Or are they feelings that are somehow inhibited, feelings that are not experienced genuinely, but only registered by a consciousness as it were in retreat – maybe merely as information? Despite their apparent ineffability, there is a contradiction implicit in Jameson's refusal to give form to them. They can, it would seem, according to his two pronouncements, simultaneously be 'dominated by a peculiar type of euphoria' whilst offering us no clues to meaning, in the way that their predecessors did. Is not Jameson merely substituting the category of euphoria for that of anxiety whilst trying to conceal the motives for such a substitution in seeking the semantic asylum of the ineffable? Needless to say, of the two categories, it is undoubtedly the latter that appeals to Jameson's nostalgic and romantic conception of authentic creative achievement. Great art, the loss of which he so clearly laments, has after all rarely been founded on the pleasure principle.

The nostalgia mode

The transition from modernist styles to postmodern codes has not only robbed us of the possibility of 'personal expression', at least as it has until recently been understood, but it has also deeply problematised our relationship to the past and therefore our self-understanding as part of an historical continuum. As a result, contemporary society, as we learn from Jameson, 'reflects not only the absence of any collective project, but also the unavailability of the older national language itself'.[14] But what exactly has been lost? Are not constructs such as the mythic national language and collective projects, to which Jameson refers, part of exactly the sort of modernist narrative projects that postmodernism contests on the basis of their homogenisation, logocentrism, representational monopolisation and refusal of difference? In other words all the narrative legitimations that Lyotard (*Postmodern Condition*) finds lacking or discredited. Transcendent masterpieces and 'great' men/artists may well now be things of the past, but I can imagine few people mourning the loss of the older collective language of racism, phallocentrism and class domination that conferred upon it the appearance of univocality – the 'national' of Jameson's language and the spurious 'collectivity' of his projects. Granted therefore that the object of loss is itself a mythical construct, and in that sense can never be recovered, what Jameson is really bemoaning is perhaps the loss of a common national language, not for its own sake, but rather as a monolith against which individual attitudes and values can stand out. Once again, it would appear that the 'authentic' alternative to a culture of 'sheer heterogeneity' and 'random difference' being promoted is, in fact, a modernism associated not with avant-gardism but with romanticism.

With the crisis of confidence in the depth models of modernism we have come to inhabit an era dominated by categories of space rather than time. Our mode of experiencing the world has shifted from the diachronic to the synchronic in which, in Jameson's words, 'the retrospective dimension indispensable to any vital reorientation of our collective future – has meanwhile itself become a vast collection of images, a multitudinous photographic simulacrum'.[15] This has become most tangibly evident in terms of the rampant museification of culture that has gone hand in hand with the commodification of the past. History has now become heritage,[16] the theme park displacing the museum and library as repositories of historical knowledge and bringing with it a whole new ecology of fantasy, nostalgia and desire that finds its apotheosis in the ahistory of the Disney World experience.

The 'new spatial logic of the simulacrum' displaces the past as meaningful 'referent', substituting instead a polysemous textuality. This textuality is the 'debris' that we sift through in an attempt to secure our place in history, to construct for ourselves a culture that is more than simply a parody of lost forms. Jameson's analysis of Doctorow's *Ragtime* is intended to illustrate exactly this – 'the fate of real history' – the way in which the 'retrospective dimension' is never anything more than the representation of our ideas and stereotypes about the past. But what is really being lamented in this analysis is not 'the fate of real history' – after all 'real history' no more than 'national language' ever existed independent of its analysis – but the effacement of the distinction between 'real' history and 'pop' history. Again it is 'authenticity' that is at stake as the reality principle is progressively undermined.

Cultural production is therefore driven back inside a mental space which is no longer that of the old monadic subject, but rather that of some degraded collective 'objective spirit'; it can no longer gaze directly on some putative real world, at some reconstruction of past history that was itself once a present; rather, as in Plato's cave, it must trace our mental images of that past on its confining walls.[17]

One of the manifestations of this new relation to the past is the 'nostalgia film' or 'la mode retro' that Jameson sees as witness not to the indifference but rather to the omnipresent, omnivorous and libidinal historicism that accompanies our addiction to the photographic image. As the new becomes discarded as an outmoded category and the invention of the new is abandoned as an anachronistic presumption, the past is simply treated as a repertoire of retrievable signifiers. Style itself is now defined as the reworking of the antecedent. No longer able to gain access to the past through the representation of historical content, the nostalgia film therefore attempts to appropriate a missing past and resurrect the lost referential through stylistic connotation alone. 'Pastness' has become a question of genre. Thus Kazden's film *Body Heat* is decipherable in terms of its temporal location only if one is aware of its predecessors, *Obsessione* and *The Postman Always Rings Twice*. Where films confuse or conflate genres, as for instance in a film like *Diva*, they appear to be located in a period beyond historical time which is exactly the effect that, in exaggerated form, the textuality of 'pastness' has on films that truly purport to be representative of an actual historical period. As Jameson points out,

> the preexistence of other versions . . . is now a constitutive and essential part of the film's structure: we are now, in other words, in 'intertextuality' as a built-in feature of the aesthetic effect, and as the operator of a new connotation of 'pastness' and pseudo-historical depth, in which the history of aesthetic styles displaces 'real' history.[18]

According to this view the past gains existence only at the level of signifiers of pastness which themselves have become detached from their signifieds and original denotational properties. Here the depth model based on the semiotic opposition between the signifier and the signified has been relinquished as the signifier becomes free-floating and autonomous. It is a transformation that will be examined in greater detail in relation to the work of Baudrillard.

However, the nostalgia mode cannot simply be dismissed as libidinal historicism. To describe a film such as *Star Wars* as a nostalgia movie in the sense that it metonymically recreates our Buck Rogers fantasies from the 1930s and 1940s, is only interesting as a piece of cultural analysis if it also examines the nature of the archetypes that are being revived. What Jameson's otherwise acute analysis fails to address is the political nature of contemporary nostalgic yearning for the past – in other words what exactly it is that contemporary audiences wish to feel nostalgic about. *Desert Hearts, Peggy Sue got Married, Back to the Future, Radio Days, Tucker,* etc. – all attest to the continuing success of the genre. The particular way in which experience is reinvented must be read as politically symptomatic of the formation and realisation of collective desire in terms of the rehabilitation of non-existent role models and archetypes.

The flow of the cultural capital that resides in such nostalgic recreations need not, however, be confined to the single direction described by Jameson. Nor should its apparently libidinal historicism be allowed to obscure the possibility of a hidden political agenda. The 'nostalgia mode' need not function purely retrospectively, reclaiming and reinventing (whether metonymically or otherwise) a past to which we no longer have access. It can also operate prospectively as a means of colonising in advance areas of the collective public imagination. In the appropriately titled 'Short History of the Future' series (Equinox, Channel 4), some of the machinations of the future as a self-fulfilling prophecy were revealed by establishing connections between images of the future provided by, for instance, Chesley Bonnestel and von Braun for Walt Disney's 'Tomorrowland' theme park, and the actualities of a developing space-programme that was required to fulfil the demands of a public whose expectations were already established.

Like the past, the future too is increasingly organised around the post-modern model of spatial synchrony, thereby relinquishing any claim to the temporal depth that had previously distinguished it from the lived present. The spatial logic of the simulacrum has in this sense colonised every aspect of the temporal signifier. The reinvention of the past, like the preinvention of the future, takes place according to the dictates of the consuming demands of the present. However, unlike the referent of 'pastness' for which 'the history of aesthetic styles displaces real history', the 'future' referent apparently makes no such claim to a reality principle from which it can be displaced or dislodged. The future is thus optimistically characterised in terms of the unknown.

The history of the serial (and later movies) *Star Trek*[19] is in this sense paradigmatic. Kirk, Spock and the rest of the *Star Trek* crew promise 'to explore strange new worlds, to seek out new life and new civilisations' and in the immortal words of the space frontier language that has sustained the American space programme ever since, 'To boldly go where no man has gone before.' Significantly, *Star Trek* only really gained popularity after the Apollo mission reruns (from 1972 onwards) saw audience ratings drop, requiring a reinvention of the future referent. Fact was predictably enough reinvented according to fiction in September 1976, when the newly developed shuttle orbiter was, after much petitioning (from the 'public' as well as baptised 'Trekkies') named the USS *Enterprise*, and wheeled out to be greeted by the Skylab space-team, the *Star Trek* team and President Reagan. The merging of fact and fiction (which had, of course, always been former President Reagan's strongest asset), the duplication of the space teams, was sufficient to render both artificial, thus diverting attention from the economic burden of its funding. Extensive NASA collaboration in later films, *2001 Space Odyssey*, *Star Trek the Motion Picture* (for which Jesco von Putthamer, the NASA consultant, wrote much of the script) and of course *Star Wars*, confirm the degree to which the signifiers of the future, divorced from their temporal referent, become active in the recreation of the present in reverse. In an ironic inversion of what Jameson describes as the 'nostalgia mode', the future, seen as the history of aesthetic styles, becomes rather than displaces 'real' history, which, in a Baudrillardian spiral of sameness, cyclically reverts to its starting point as an aesthetic style.

In an interesting article entitled, 'From Here to Modernity: Feminism and Postmodernism', published in the postmodern edition of *Screen*,[20] Barbara Creed approaches the 'nostalgia' debate in a different way by asking whether it takes a different form for men and women. Creed identifies two different forms of nostalgia film referred to by Jameson – the period recreation and the adventure film – both of which invoke an absent symbolic order though in radically different ways. According to her, the intensely polarised gender roles of the adventure film – *Raiders of the Lost Ark* being an obvious example – invoke a desire to relive a mythical time when gender roles were more stable and clearly defined – or as Gil Scott Heron put it in a different context, to 'a time when heroes weren't zeros and real men could die with their boots on'. Where Jameson's account of the nostalgic tendency falls short, from Creed's point of view, is that he situates the 'older period' literally in the past – specifically the Saturday afternoon serial of the 1930s and 1950s with its alien villains, true American heroes and heroines in distress – and fails to consider 'the possibility that all generations may have similar longings (although often tempered with cynicism), and that the cinema, along with other forms of popular culture, addresses these longings in different ways and through different filmic modes across the decades'.[21]

It is the failure adequately to address questions of desire and the construction of sexual difference in the cinema that is also the criticism levelled at the other type of 'nostalgia film' discussed by Jameson, the period recreation. The way in which this type of film reconstructs types of patriarchal order is the subject of the rest of Creed's critique. In drawing our attention to the issue of gender and thus insisting on the political nature of our nostalgic desires, an important point is made regarding methodology. For, although Jameson's article is never anything but lucid and insightful, the apparent neutrality of its descriptive tone masks a nostalgic subtext that is itself, theoretically rather than filmically, 'a la mode retro'.

Desperately seeking diachrony

With the dissolution of narrative or linear time, history and reality assume the form of discontinuous fragments that jostle and collide in a chaotic Brownian motion of isolated and sovereign moments. Information no longer conforms to the suteral chains of the ordered narratives. Refusing organisation within the filing system of historical narrative, it now accumulates with a blithe disregard for the 'great' modernist imperatives of order and reason. Instead it is exponential, viral and engulfing. It has become the wreckage that threatens to destroy Walter Benjamin's famous angel of history:

> This is how one pictures the angel of history. His face is turned towards the past. Where we perceive a chain of events, he sees one single catastrophe which keeps piling wreckage upon wreckage and hurls it in front of his feet. The angel would like to stay, awaken the dead and make whole what has been smashed. But a storm is blowing from Paradise; it has got caught in his wings with such violence that the angel can no longer close them. This storm irresistibly propels him into the future to which his back is turned, while the pile of debris before him grows skyward. This storm is what we call progress.[22]

Benjamin's allegory is particularly resonant in an age for which it is the individual as well as the angel who finds him/herself rummaging, perplexed, among the debris. Seeking moments of stability and perspective from within the chaotic and contradictory violence of the present we increasingly find ourselves seeking refuge in nostalgia – in a vision of the past from which the worst wrinkles of contradiction have been ironed out, in a past that has been domesticated to suit the desperate needs of the present. Like much of the writing to come out of the Frankfurt school, which so clearly informs Jameson's account of postmodernism, Benjamin's work participates in this nostalgia for the era before the storm.

'When the real is no longer what it used to be, nostalgia assumes its full meaning',[23] writes Baudrillard. Nostalgia also assumes that there was once a stable exchange between meaning and the real, when both had their designated place in the order of things. It is in this sense that Jameson's 'critique' of postmodernism is itself, like Adorno's attack on the 'culture industry' (also from the Frankfurt school), in the 'nostalgia mode' – a nostalgia for a culture that could accommodate oppositional positions of an easily identifiable sort. But it is exactly these neat binary oppositions that postmodernism discards. As has already been established, the cornerstone of Jameson's defence of what he calls the 'high modernists' is a fascination with the then still operative category of personal expression that is so profoundly problematised within the context of postmodernism. The obsession with absolute uniqueness of self and of style is the expression of a desire to relive, or at least revitalise, an imaginary order of the defined, stable and predictable social relations of a reality principle unthreatened by the mutability of the simulacra.

Jameson introduced the discussion of postmodernism by attempting to situate it against the 'cultural logic' or 'hegemonic norm' of late capitalism. In condemning commodification, Jameson's rejection of postmodernism is simultaneously a rejection of popular culture. In this sense his analysis corresponds closely to that of another critic, also writing from the 'left' – his English counterpart, Terry Eagleton.

In *Against the Grain* Eagleton praises modernism for resisting commodification, thereby retaining a claim to 'authenticity' and the attendant categories of 'personal expression' valorised by Jameson. Eagleton contrasts it with a postmodernist culture which will 'dissolve its own boundaries and become coextensive with ordinary commodified life itself'.[24] The dissolution of the 'semi-autonomy' (to use Marcuse's phrase) of the cultural sphere by the logic of late capital is also described by Jameson, interestingly characterised in terms of explosion rather than implosion;

> A prodigious expansion of culture throughout the social realm, to the point at which everything in our social life – from economic value and state power to practices and to the very structure of the psyche itself – can be said to have become 'cultural' in some original and as yet untheorised sense.[25]

But, despite the repeated claim that it is the reterritorialisation of capital that has resulted in the total acculturation of all aspects of social life, it is the centring power of (romantic) modernism, rather than the decentring power of late capitalism, that is actually being examined. Thus although postmodernism problematises modernist notions of the centred subject, it does not, as Jameson is forced to maintain, necessarily lead to its death.

To quote James Collins writing for *Screen*; 'While a unitary culture may have disappeared, unitary discourses constructing very specific subjects have only intensified. The category of subject remains highly viable in part because it has never been so hotly contested.'[26] Theories of subjectivity, introduced by Jameson's account of schizophrenia, will be the subject of the next chapter.

Notes

1 Frederic Jameson, 'The Cultural Logic of Late Capitalism', *New Left Review*, no.146, July/Aug 1984. Also published in a shorter version as 'Postmodernism and Consumer Society' in Hal Foster (ed.), *Postmodern Culture* (Pluto Press, 1985).

2 See Ernest Mandel, *Late Capitalism* (New Left Books, 1976). For a lengthy and useful review of this work see 'Late Capitalism' by Bob Rowthorn in *New Left Review*, no. 98, July/Aug 1976.

3 Jameson, 'The Cultural Logic of Late Capitalism', p.78.

4 Ibid., p.57.

5 Jean-François Lyotard, *The Postmodern Condition: A Report on Knowledge* (Manchester University Press, 1984) p.76.

6 Dan Latimer, 'Jameson and Postmodernism', *New Left Review*, no.147, 1984/5.
7 Jameson, 'The Cultural Logic of Late Capitalism', p.58.
8 Ibid., p.61.
9 Guy Debord, *Society of the Spectacle* (Red and Black, 1983).
10 See Judy and Fred Vermorel, *Starlust* (1987).
11 Jameson, 'The Cultural Logic of Late Capitalism', p.65.
12 Ibid., p.64.
13 See Bernard Blistine, 'A Conversation with Jean-François Lyotard', *Flash Art*, no.121, March 1985, p.65.
14 Jameson, 'The Cultural Logic of Late Capitalism', p.65.
15 Ibid., p.66.
16 See Richard Hewison, *The Heritage Industry* (Verso, 1988).
17 Jameson, 'The Cultural Logic of Late Capitalism', p.71.
18 Ibid., p.67.
19 For a history of *Star Trek* and the evolution of episodes see Gary Geran and Paul H. Schulman's *Fantastic Television: A Pictorial History of Sci-Fi, the Unusual and the Fantastic, from the 50s to the 70s* (Titan, 1987).
20 Barbara Creed, 'From Here to Modernity: Feminism and Post-modernism', *Screen*, vol.28, no.2, Spring 1987.
21 Ibid., p.54.
22 Walter Benjamin, *Illuminations* (Fontana, 1973) pp. 259–60.
23 Jean Baudrillard, *Simulations*, (Semiotext(e), 1984) p.12.
24 Terry Eagleton, *Against the Grain: Capitalism, Modernism and Post-modernism* (Verso, 1986) p.141.
25 Jameson, 'The Cultural Logic of Late Capitalism', p.87.
26 James Collins, 'Postmodernism and Cultural Practice', *Screen*, vol. 28, no.2, Spring 1987, p.24.

5 Doubletalk

> The post-modern subject must live with the fact that not only are its languages arbitrary, but it is itself an 'effect' of language, a precipitate of the very symbolic order of which the humanist subject supposed itself to be master.
>
> Victor Burgin, *The End of Art Theory*

With semiology and structural linguistics finally gaining curricular legitimacy within the academy, a degree of familiarity can, I think, be assumed. With the delivery of his course in general linguistics between 1907 and 1911, Saussure broke with mainstream Anglo-Saxon thought by defining man in terms of his outward language rather than by his inward powers of mind. As a scientist, Saussure argued that the down-to-earth reality of speech should take precedence over the idealised propriety of writing. At the same time he argued that *langue* should take precedence over *parole*, in other words that the system of language in general should take precedence over the sum total of the utterances ever actually uttered. *Langue*, the abstract underlying system of language, thus became the object of systematic study, while *parole* was left outside such study, as the supposedly free-willed act of personal expression. In this way he attacked the nominalist account of language according to which the sign is assumed to be 'transparent', allowing unproblematic access to the referent.

Saussure's sign, upon which his account of language is based, is a 'two-sided psychological entity' consisting of a sound-image (signifier) and concept (signified). In his words:

> The linguistic sign unites not a thing and a name but a concept and a sound-image. The latter is not the material sound, a purely physical thing, but the psychological imprint of the sound, the impression that it makes on our senses. The sound-image is sensory, and if I happen to call it 'material' it is only in that sense, and by way of opposing it to the other term in the association, the concept, which is generally more abstract.[1]

To speak of concepts is now to imply differentiation and a logic of differentiation that for Saussure is not specific or material, but abstract. Concepts are no longer defined simply by content – a definition which saw

72

content belonging to an *external* and therefore objective world separate from, but juxtaposed to, the *internal* world of the subjective mind – but also, and primarily, by their oppositional relationships with other concepts. Understanding the sign now requires a sort of tripartite background: there must of course be a speaker and a listener, but there must also be an interpretant, another sign or body of signs which is either concurrent with the sign in question, or present in memory, and which may be substituted for it.

As a means of explicating this account of language, the well-known chess analogy provides illumination. From the point of view of someone who had no familiarity with the game it might seem obvious that one should study chess in terms of the sum total of all the moves in all the games that have ever been played. But this would fail to account for chess as a game unless one was to understand that each individual move is selected simply as one option from a much larger range of possible moves. No single move is significant, except in relation to what has preceded it and of course to the projected strategy of moves that may follow. Such strategy is predictive, determined at least in part by the player's anticipation of his/her opponent's response. To study chess properly one must therefore look at the simultaneous system of principles for making moves – the simultaneous system that lies behind every move at every point in the game. This system precedes any actual moves. Like language it must be internalised in its entirety, in terms of its structural coherence rather than its individual parts. Where the structure is common, the moves are not. Only when both players have internalised this structure does the game become meaningful.

What the chess analogy reveals is a conception of language as a structure of differentiation. It is a system with no positive terms, based as it is on the categorical denial of the possibility of positive entities. Because of this the unity of the sign, the bond forged between any given signifier and signified, is comprehensible only from the standpoint of language conceived synchronically, as a closed system, where its meaning is fixed in relation to a totality of other signs. This structure, like the rules of chess, needs to be internalised and shared if the system is to operate with any degree of success. No single person can create new words and meanings: 'langue' must always be shared. To make sense, individual words must belong to what Saussure terms 'the common storehouse of language'. This storehouse is a pre-existent *social* reality, and one that is shared ultimately by the whole of society. In Saussure's words: '[langue] is the social side of speech, outside the individual who can never create or modify it by himself; it exists only by virtue of a sort of contract signed by the members of the community'.[2] But the use of the term 'contract' is somewhat misleading, since it is a contract that cannot be evaluated any more than it can be said to be born of agreement or negotiation. We cannot understand or realise the implications until they are upon us. This is because words and meanings are, as Richard Harland puts it, 'deposited in the individual's brain below the level of conscious ownership and mastery. They lie within him like an undigested piece of society'.[3]

In attacking the traditional Anglo-Saxon account of meaning as generated from the one-to-one relationship between signifier and signified, between the materiality of a word and its concept, Saussure repositions language in relation to society. The signifier takes on the aspect of a social reality as opposed to a subjective event. What is important to the process of signification is that the same structure of formal relationships is preserved. However this principle of differentiation applies equally to signifieds. Although signifieds are concepts, they have nothing to do with the traditional way of conceiving them in terms of images, mirrorings or mental 'things'. 'The concepts are purely differential and defined not by their positive content but negatively by their relations with other terms of the system. Their most precise characteristic is in being what the others are not.'[4]

By way of elucidation I shall summarise Richard Harland's account of the functioning of the concept signified, according to his example, by the word 'rape'. This choice of word/concept is particularly appropriate since the structurally relational character of the meaning of 'rape' has been especially highlighted ever since feminists began talking about 'rape within marriage'. Why this combination of meaning has proved so hard for society to accept has little to do with the terrifying reality of sex-by-force, which may be equally brutal and humiliating inside or outside the institution of marriage. Rather the meaning of the word is dependent upon the institutionalised opposition between the meaning of 'rape' and the meaning of 'marriage'. What 'marriage' is, 'rape' is not: in Harland's words, 'approval and legality polarised against abhorrence and criminality'.[5] With the concept redefined in terms of differentiation we now have to map the functions of language across a different axis: no longer paired on a vertical axis – the signifier being above but transparent to the signified below it – language must now be seen to operate horizontally across the two-dimensional space of differentiation.

Saussure therefore conceives of language as 'a system whose parts can and must all be considered in their synchronic solidarity'.[6] Meaning, according to this view, is generated not from the movement from signifier to signified, but from signifier to signifier. What we generally call the signified – the meaning or conceptual content of an utterance – is henceforth regarded as a meaning-effect, as the objective mirage of signification generated and projected by the relationship of signifiers among each other. The significance of this shift in emphasis is that the human being can no longer be regarded as the centred subject of his or her various representations since he or she is now an *effect* of the signifier rather than the cause. It is an inversion that predicates Lacan's account of subjectivity and that permeates virtually every aspect of postmodern discourse.

For the schizophrenic this inversion is not a deconstructive strategy devised in order to destabilise the humanist subject of *ancien regime* academics – it is to a varying degree lived, experienced and suffered. But it also seems to be rooted in a specifically linguistic failure – the failure to grasp language in terms of its 'synchronic solidarity'. Words and meanings, the 'undigested pieces of society' that 'exist below the level of conscious ownership and mastery', for the schizophrenic become indigestible. Unable to locate them within a shared structure of differentiation and meaning he or she is denied access to society's collective meanings leaving only the experience of the isolated signifier in its state of pure materiality. The schizophrenic becomes like the monad who is unable to escape the shadow of his/her own formula in confrontation with a stream of accumulating signifiers which, like ill-fitting jigsaw-pieces, refuse to take their designated place on the plane of 'synchronic solidarity', refusing assimilation within the structure that is greater than themselves – namely language. It is out of this background that Jameson rather curiously proposes the experience of the schizophrenic as forming the basis of a 'suggestive aesthetic model' that corresponds to our postmodern condition.

Lacan: selfhood, the imaginary and the symbolic

Having summarised the contribution made by Saussure to our conception of the operations of language, we must now turn to Lacan if we are to understand the relationship being proposed between schizophrenic subjectivity and the (de)structuring of experience within language. Lacan's most obvious debt to Saussure is in his reformulation of the thinking unconscious as a functioning sign-system of empty structural differentiations. In his famous phrase, 'the unconscious is structured like language'.[7]

Such a claim, although apparently alien to the Anglo-Saxon tradition of pschoanalysis, with its rigid alignment of the unconscious and the instincts and biological needs of the human species, is in fact based on an analytical *rereading* of the early Freud. The force of the connection between the unconscious and basic instinct is, according to Lacan, the product of mistranslation. Freud's English translators tended to imply a necessary connection between the unconscious and the instincts through the mistranslation of 'trieb' as 'instinct', whereas Freud deliberately reserved the word 'instinkt' to talk about instincts. 'Trieb', physical drives or pulsions, may be quite unconnected. The distinction is important. In connecting the unconscious with a biological notion of what is instinctual, the Anglo-Saxon interpretation is committed to conceptualising it in terms of sensory images – concrete, 'primitive' and preconceptual – since instincts and biological needs can themselves be appeased only through the senses. The latent assumption behind such an interpretation is that whatever is underlying and basic can only be underlying and basic in the way that biology is underlying and basic. Lacan resists relapsing into the behaviourism of the traditional Anglo-Saxon interpretation, emphasising instead the way in which the unconscious is penetrated and structured according to the socialising and differential determinations of language: 'the unconscious is neither primordial nor instinctual; what it knows about the elementary is no more than the elements of the signifier.'[8]

Lacan's 'return to Freud', is a return to the early Freud of *The Interpretation of Dreams*, *The Psychopathology of Everyday Life* and *Jokes and the Unconscious*, in which the model of psyche is formulated around the conscious, pre-conscious and unconscious, rather than the later work in which it was superseded by the triadical model of the id, ego and super-ego. According to this later schema, the ego's capacity to maintain its identity depends on its ability to sort out the conflicts that arise from the drives of unconscious impulses (id) for free expression and the demands of conscience (superego) for their renunciation. The repression of instinctual desires pressed upon the ego by the id allows the energy of the impulses denied to be sublimated in creative endeavour – the self is here seen in terms of its response to or resolution of internal contradictions rather than external impositions. From the later Freud, and specifically the ego-analysts reading of this work, we develop a conception of the self formed, as it were, from within rather than from without. But, as Lacan insists: Freud's unconscience is not at all the romantic unconscience of imaginative creation. It is not the locus of the divinities of the night.'[9]

The basis for Lacan's preference for the earlier model proposed by Freud is therefore that it rid him of the suggestion of individual selfhood that the term ego automatically supposes – as the sense of being an individual self is unnecessary to the conscious or pre-conscious and untrue to the unconscious. The early work of Freud allowed for a conception of selfhood that need not necessarily be a function of its proximity to some unspecified behaviouristic norm. Lacan's rereading of Freud, in particular the work done in collaboration with Breuer whilst experimenting with the technique of hypnosis, showed him that in the unconscious, society and the 'other' have already preceded the individuality and selfhood that is the subject of ego-analysis. Individual selfhood is therefore no longer conceptualised in terms of healthy growth or natural extension but as 'meconnaissance', imposed and extraneous – what he terms a paranoid construct. (Deleuze and Guatteri later extended this notion of 'meconnaisance' to include a critique of the whole Oedipalising foundation of psychoanalysis, itself redefined as a self-perpetuating paranoid construct: 'Oedipus is first the idea of an adult paranoiac, before it is the childhood feeling of a neurotic . . . Guilt is an idea projected by the father before it is an inner feeling experienced by the son. The first error of psychoanalysis is in acting as if things began with the child.'[10]) In terms of the psychoanalytical cure, developed notions of selfhood become an active hindrance, to be overcome rather than developed; 'In my experience the ego represents the centre to all resistances to the treatment of symptons.'[11]

Barriers are erected between the patient and analyst for the same reasons – the resistance of the ego being most commonly encapsulated in the enunciation; 'I can't bear the thought of being freed by anyone other than myself.'[12]

Freud's early experiments with hypnosis gave Lacan the first indication of what he was later to term 'the discourse of the other'. As a technique devised to reach levels of the mind below consciousness, hypnosis was, it was thought, dependent on concentration-on-an-object – in the mesmeric tradition, the hypnotist's eyes. However, in rethinking hypnotic techniques it becomes clear that the concentration-on-an-object, formerly thought to be a crucial factor in its effectivity, works only as a means of reducing background stimuli, and that hypnosis works primarily through verbal suggestion. The unconscious that hypnosis reveals is therefore an unconscious that answers to language. The stage exploitation of hypnosis, when, for instance, the volunteer is induced to eat a lemon that is interpreted and sensually enjoyed as an apple, also demonstrates the way in which linguistic interpretation can no longer be thought of as merely a superstructure founded on a base of sensory perception. The response of the subject under hypnosis is therefore that of one who has been 'taken over' by an implanted 'interpretive connection'. This interpretive connection is dependent upon a myth from the outside which Lacan terms 'the discourse of the other'.[13]

In the *Ecrits*, Lacan attempts to situate the incursion of language in terms of the successive phases of the child's development. The 'false' construction of the self is explained in two stages. The first stage occurs from the age of six months onwards when the child becomes aware of its own image in the mirror. The child's fascination with the image that it recognises as its own, is the fascination with a self whose 'reality' is derived not from its reproducibility, but rather, to recontextualise Baudrillard's phrase, from the fact that it is always already reproduced. The image that the child sees is also the image of what the child aspires to be, as throughout the 'mirror phase' the image of the body is seen from the outside – the image of a unified coherent self separated from the rest of the world.

The child's initial experience of the self is essentially open-ended, exploratory and unfocused – an experience that corresponds to the stage of sexual development which is polymorphously perverse. But at the moment of self-recognition (the mirror phase) the child recuperates the totality of his/her body in an image and gradually becomes conscious of his/her self as an entity. This narcissistic fascination with the image is due to what Lacan terms 'prematurity of birth' or 'primordial discord'[14] and is seen as a compensatory device for the actual disunity and incoherence of the self experienced by the child. In identifying with its own image, seen from the outside in the gaze of the other, the child restores to itself the unity and coherence that is absent from its actual experience of the self:

The mirror stage is interesting in that it manifests the affective dynamism by which the subject originally identifies himself with the *Gestalt* of his own body: in relation to the still very profound lack of co-ordination of his own motility, it represents an ideal unity, a salutary *imago*; it is invested with all the original distress resulting from the child's interorganic and relational discordance.[15]

However this first dual relationship between the child and its like – its own image reflected in the mirror, the mother herself or her substitutes – does not provide the child with 'subjectivity' in the sense of the singularity given to that term. It may register a totality that compensates for the lived experience of fragmentation, but in becoming his own double more than he is himself the narcissism of the mirror phase automatically situates the instance of the ego in the line of fiction. It is also the line of alienation, since alienation, according to Anika Lemaire, is the fact of giving up a part of oneself to another: 'The alienated man lives outside himself, a prisoner of the signifier, a prisoner of the ego's image or of the image of the ideal. He lives by the other's gaze upon him and he is unaware of this.'[16]

The second phase of the child's development occurs from the age of 18 months onwards, when through verbalisation the child enters into society and society's language enters into the child. This is the point at which language and social laws begin to determine the subject and form him/her in accordance with their own characteristics. The mirror stage prefigures this second stage, which also depends on the acquired double-sided mechanisms that initiate the dialectic between alienation and subjectivity, the self and the 'other'. For on one side, language belongs to society – to return to Saussure: 'it exists only by virtue of a sort of contract signed by the members of the community'[17] – but because the contract allows no room for negotiation, the child, in order to acquire language, must surrender something of the self and speak from the position of the 'other'.

However, from the other side, when the child speaks of the self from the position of the 'other', this self, like the self of the mirror phase, seen from the outside in the gaze of the 'other', is more unified and coherent than ever actually experienced. To enter into society's language is to enter into a personal name and personal pronoun as to speak of the self in society's language is to speak in terms of 'me', 'myself' and 'I'. The paradox of the mirror phase thus extends to the language phase – that the individual self derives not from the progressive discovery or externalisation of some real inner sense of self, but from the 'other', from outside. Thus, it is only when the child, who previously had existed only as a polymorphous, uncoordinated being, is invited to identify his/her self from the point of view of the other, that identity is constructed as an 'imaginary' image.

The 'Imaginary' order is not however a sufficient precondition of singularity. Coherent notions of selfhood can only emerge with the subject's entry into the symbolic order: 'The subject is born insofar as the signifier emerges in the field of the Other. But by this very fact, this subject – which was previously nothing if not a subject coming into being – solidifies into a signifier.' A central role in this process of solidification is played by the Oedipus complex whereby the subject accepts a position in terms of sexual difference. In a patriarchal society this involves acknowledgement of the primacy of the masculine position; the symbolic phallus and the 'Law of the Father'. This process exists as one of continual transition. Unlike the later interpellated subject proposed by Althusser, which occupies a singular position in relation to ideology, the Lacanian subject is constantly recreated and reformed in the syncope or gap between the experiential self and the 'other'.

For Lacan, the subject-of-the-enunciation and the subject-of-the-enounced are never fully correlated and the 'suture' or stitching of the subject to the other, the symbolic order, is never final. It is always in process, motivated by a desire which is unsatisfiable. For the child who acquires language in order to request and demand, desire can no longer be conceptualised simply in terms of self-interest, since the 'other' of language is also the perspective of the 'other' upon the 'I'. It is in this sense that Lacan writes that, 'narcissism envelops the form of the desire.'[18] Gratification can only be sought from the perspective of the 'other' on the 'I', so that as desire is refracted in the mirror of the 'other', satisfiable need becomes lost in a demand for love and admiration: desire can never be one's own and the selfhood that it wishes to confirm is itself chimerical.

Lacan's account of subjectivity, or more specifically the double-sided mechanisms according to which the subject is formed, represents a vital convergence of the discoveries of structural anthropology, linguistics and psychoanalysis. Insisting upon the fact that sociocultural and linguistic symbolisms impose themselves as structures before the emerging (child) subject makes his or her entry into them, Lacan offers a route to understanding some of the pathologies that have become associated with, and representative of, our present postmodern condition. It is a route through which we can perhaps begin to understand the suffering that such pathologies cause. That understanding must begin by discarding our inherited nineteenth-century notions of the centred individual as the perpetrator of his or her own suffering.

Schizophrenia: Jameson's 'suggestive aesthetic model'

With this conjunction of structural linguistics and Freudian psychoanalysis, we can, following Lacan, begin to develop a conception of subjectivity no longer grounded in the 'natural' or behaviouristic sciences. The unity or disunity of the self is no longer a function of its proximity to some inherent biological norm, but is rather seen to be an effect of its constantly changing construction within language. The nominalist model, whether seen in its linguistic or 'psychological' dimensions, is therefore inadequate as an account of a fugitive subjectivity, the coherence of which is in the constantly paradoxical state of being destroyed as it is defined.

The breakdown of the signifying chain can, accordingly, no longer be distinguished from the emergence of a correspondingly 'broken down' or disjunctive subjectivity. It is this observation, informed by Lacanian psychoanalytic theory, that has led Jameson to make the important comparison between the disappearance of the unified ego in postmodernism and the fragmentation of the self in the schizophrenic condition. The dispersal of subjectivity across the spatial and synchronic field of postmodern experience can now be understood in terms of an inability to unify the self in the 'other' of language. What Lacan makes clear is that even before birth the individual is caught up in and completely assimilated into a causal chain of which s/he can never be any more than an effect. The interlocking series of signifiers which had hitherto constituted an utterance or meaning are experienced in a way that prohibits the adoption of the definitive subject positions that gave the self, as bourgeois monad, the illusion of mastery and control. With the breakdown of the signifying chain, signifiers are experienced in their 'pure' form as autonomous units, no longer anchored to their referential 'reality'. Similarly the self, whose coherence was dependent upon the ability to connect the signifier and the signified – a process which effects entry into the symbolic order as well as fashioning the subject in accordance with the structures (linguistic and Oedipal) proper to that order – is, following this breakdown, experienced as free-floating and mutable. According to Jameson the connection between this kind of linguistic malfunction and the psyche of the schizophrenic may be grasped by way of the following two-fold proposition; 'first, that personal identity is itself the effect of a certain temporal unification of past and present with the present before me; and second, that such active temporal unification is itself a function of language, or better still of the sentence, as it moves along its hermeneutic circle in time.'[19] As he goes on to point out, the failure to unify the past, present and future of a sentence must, following Lacan, result in a similar inability in terms of our own biographical experience or psychic life.

So much for the theory – though the example of this in 'practice' is somewhat less digestible. In order to describe the nature of this new type of 'schizophrenic' experience Jameson quotes extensively from the opening paragraph of the first page of the celebrated *Autobiography of a Schizophrenic Girl*,[20] written by the unfortunate Renée and prefaced by her analyst Marguerite Sechehaye, who also provides an interpretation. (Sechehaye's own familiarity with structural linguistics and through it the work of Lacan can be assumed, since it was her husband who edited the first major translation of Saussure's *Course in General Linguistics*, thus making Jameson's selection particularly appropriate in terms of the type of answer that he wished to elicit.) The choice of passage is significant and worth relating in full:

I remember very well the day it happened. We were staying in the country and I had gone for a long walk alone as I did now and then. Suddenly as I was passing the school, I heard a German song: the children were having a singing lesson. I stopped to listen, and at that instant a strange feeling came over me, a feeling hard to analyse but akin to something I was to know too well later – a disturbing sense of unreality. It seemed to me that I no longer recognised the school, it had become as large as a barracks: the singing children were prisoners compelled to sing. It was as though the school and the children's song were set apart from the rest of the world. At the same time my eye encountered a field of wheat whose limits I could not see. The yellow vastness, dazzling in the sun, bound up with the song of the children imprisoned in the smooth stone school barracks, filled me with such anxiety that I broke into sobs. I ran home to our garden and began to play 'to make things seem as they usually were', that is, to return to reality. It was the first appearance of those elements which were always present in later sensations of unreality: illimitable vastness, brilliant light, and the gloss and smoothness of material things.[21]

For Jameson, this passage, and the sentiments that it describes, correspond uncannily to the contemporary (postmodern) experience of what he terms the fragmentation of the self. Renée's schizophrenia is taken to be symptomatic of a type of experience taken at the level of culture in general. However, before analysing the particularities of why he believes this to be the case, one should be aware of the similarities between the passage quoted and the autobiographical accounts of Van Gogh's experiences, related in his letters to his brother Theo. What is it therefore that makes the experiences recounted by Renée specifically postmodern and in some way qualitatively different from those that we associate with, for instance, Van Gogh and other great figures who supposedly epitomise the 'age of anxiety'? To a certain extent Jameson provides us with an answer. The breakdown of temporality that he identifies as being central to the schizophrenic's way of experiencing the world, in his own words, 'releases the present of time from all the activities and intentionalities that might focus it and make it a space of praxis; thereby isolated, that present suddenly engulfs the subject with undescribable vividness, a materiality of perception properly overwhelming, which effectively dramatises the power of the material – or better still, the literal – Signifier in isolation.'[22] However, the experience of the pure material signifier that characterises the schizophrenic condition is associated primarily with a 'euphoria' that replaces the older effects of anxiety and alienation. This, Jameson goes on to claim, applies equally to the girl's experience, 'which one could just as well imagine in the positive terms of euphoria'. Yet anyone who has read the whole book will see that this characterisation will not do. It is a tragic story of fear and dislocation, which Renée herself narrates in terms that are almost totally malign: 'in the midst of desolation, in indescribable distress, in absolute solitude, I am terrifyingly alone.'[23] As she graphically records the 'devastating tempest' that 'ravaged my soul',[24] the reader is left with the powerful impression that this autobiography could just as well be ranked alongside Munch's 'Scream', considered by Jameson to be the 'canonical expression of the great modernist thematics of alienation, anomie, solitude and social fragmentation and isolation, a virtually programmatic emblem of what used to be called the age of anxiety'.[25] Why then, has a work that seems so suggestive of the modernist view of the world been coopted within the orbit of the postmodern?

The answer, I would like to suggest, lies largely in Jameson's own antagonism towards, and even disdain for, the so-called schizophrenisation of postmodern experience. The 'schizophrenic' refusal to situate the self as the centred subject of history renders inarticulate those discourses that privilege one account of experience over another, and that provide the basis of Jameson's attempt to reclaim an 'authentic' cultural practice. His conception of schizophrenia as 'an aesthetic model' is therefore negative in that it is motivated throughout by a sense of loss. Following Deleuze and Guattari, I would like briefly to present the case for a positive schizophrenisation of experience as an attempt to establish more heterogeneous and mobile relationships in which the unconscious could detach itself from the family structure of capitalism and act as a fund of new thoughts, desires, networks of social organisation and revolutionary change.

Notes

1 Ferdinand de Saussure, *Course in General Linguistics* (McGraw-Hill, 1966) p.66.
2 Ibid. (in Bally/Sechehaye ed.) p.14.
3 Richard Harland, *Superstructuralism: The Philosophy of Structuralism and Poststructuralism* (Methuen, 1987) p.13.
4 Saussure, *Course in General Linguistics*, p.117.
5 Harland, *Superstructuralism*, p.16.
6 Saussure, *Course in General Linguistics*, p.87.
7 Jacques Lacan, *Four Fundamental Concepts of Psychoanalysis*, Trans. Sheridan (1977).
8 Jacques Lacan, 'The Insistence of the Letter in the Unconscious' in *The Structuralists: From Marx to Levi-Strauss*, ed. Rachel and Gorge (Doubleday, 1972) p.316.
9 Lacan, *Four Fundamental Concepts*, p.24.
10 Deleuze and Guattari, *Anti-Oedipus* (Viking Press, 1977) pp.274–5.
11 Jacques Lacan, *Ecrits: A Selection*, trans. Alan Sheridan (Tavistock, 1977) p.23.
12 Ibid., p.23.
13 Jacques Lacan, *The Language of the Self* (Delta Books, 1979) p.27.

14 Lacan, *Ecrits*, p.4.
15 Ibid., p.12.
16 Anika Lemaire, *Jacques Lacan* (Routledge and Kegan Paul, 1977) p.176.
17 Saussure, *Course in General Linguistics*, p.14.
18 Lacan, *Ecrits*, p. 137.
19 Jameson, 'The Cultural Logic of Late Capitalism', p.72.
20 Marguerite Sechehaye (ed.), *Autobiography of a Schizophrenic Girl* trans. G. Rubin-Rabson (N.Y. 1968).
21 Ibid., p.19.
22 Jameson, 'The Cultural Logic of Late Capitalism', p.74.
23 Sechehaye (ed.), *Autobiography of a Schizophrenic Girl*, p.33.
24 Ibid., p.78.
25 Jameson, 'The Cultural Logic of Late Capitalism', p.61.

6 Postpsychosis

> It is not the slumber of reason that produces monsters, but vigilant insomniac rationality.
> A schizophrenic out for a walk is a better [psychoanalytical] model than a neurotic lying on the analyst's couch ...
>
> Deleuze and Guattari, *Anti-Oedipus*

Introduction: Anti-psychiatry

R. D. Laing's *The Divided Self* and David Cooper's *The Death of the Family* were among the first English works of the anti-psychiatry movement to suggest that the fragmented personality may possess a superior truth, both resulting from, yet reapplicable to, the world of the isolated nuclear family and the manic commodity culture of late capitalism. In exploring the psychological weapons of constriction, deprivation, splitting and projection that produce the symptoms of analysis, Laing and Cooper succeeded in casting radical doubts on the traditional view of schizophrenia as a specific illness with its own pathologies. In *The Divided Self* Laing states that 'sanity or psychosis is tested by the degree of conjunction or disjunction between two persons where the one is sane by common consent.'[1] He then proceeds to question those distancing mechanisms inscribed in the language of psychoanalysis that depersonalise certain types of subjectivity to the point whereby they only appear comprehensible in terms of what he calls the 'it-processes' of the objectified organism. Although we regard the people who experience themselves in terms of 'it-processes' – automata, robots, bits of machinery or animals – as psychiatrically abnormal, we refuse to recognise the abnormality of a theory that seeks to transmute persons into automata or animals.

The same dilemma was presented in a different way when Laing asked who presents the greater threat to society: the fighter pilot who dropped the bomb on Hiroshima or the schizophrenic who believes the bomb is inside his body? The so-called 'science of the human subject' that is the legacy of the Freudian obsession with the internal (latent) workings of the individual psyche rather than its social (manifest) operations and consequences, has inevitably tended to pathologise one, whilst virtually ignoring the other. Such a 'science' depends upon the stability of these sorts of paired oppositions. However, as distinctions between 'deviance', 'perversion', 'pathology' and 'normality' become increasingly blurred – a process which in the field of sexuality is graphically documented by Sylvère Lotringer's account of the 'curing' of sexual deviance through 'satiation therapy'[2] – so the treatment and analysis of these 'symptoms' is seen to take place against the *fantasy* of social normality. An ebbing of faith in the validity of such a fantasy as well as in the reductive and totalising ambitions of any more general theory that remains mortgaged to it, has over the past couple of decades led to a reassessment of the project of psychoanalysis and its analytical and prescriptive terms. As we become less and less clear as to whether such founding terms as the unconscious can in fact exist outside of psychoanalysis,[3] so the demarcations that it offers – between the pathological and the normal, the centred subject and the decentred schizophrenic – begin to falter.

According to Laing, one of the fundamental problems that remains unresolved in either psychoanalytic theory or psychiatric practice, is how one can demonstrate the general human relevance and significance of the patient's condition when the words one has to use are specifically designed to circumscribe the meaning of the patient's life to a particular clinical entity. (Even Kingsley Hall, the ruleless 'anti-psychiatric' community established in 1965 by Laing and Joseph Berke, ultimately failed to escape this dilemma. The interpretive psychoanalytical/psychiatric machine it aimed to dismantle responded not by disappearing but by *extending* itself. This occurred to the point at which Mary Barnes, who had become a sort of star of madness, simply 'interpreted everything that was done for her (or for anyone else for that matter) as therapy . . . If the coal was not delivered when ordered that was therapy. And so on to the most absurd conclusions.'[4] Far from abolishing the language of treatment and treated, the Kingsley Hall experiment appears to have reimposed the very divisions that it sought to cast aside, but from as it were the 'other side', from the perspective of the 'patient'.) The vocabulary used to describe psychiatric patients is such that it splits the individual up verbally in a way that is analogous to the existential splits already experienced. In Laing's words, 'we are condemned to start our study of schizoid and schizophrenic people with a verbal and conceptual splitting that matches the split up of the totality of the schizoid being-in-the-world.'[5] Sadly, as the case of Mary Barnes seems to illustrate, it is a split which cannot be healed from 'within' – by exchanging the terms of therapy and therapist. In retaining the language, we are also committed to retaining the terms of the larger institution (of psychoanalysis if not of psychiatry) to which it responds.

A similar point is made by Foucault in *Mental Illness and Psychology* and later elaborated in *Madness and Civilisation*. He claims that in effect psychiatric 'medicine' works only to the extent that patients are persuaded into speaking about themselves in the language of science – in this case specifically the language of psychiatry. In this sense patients are designated 'mad' only because they have evaded the socialising processes – the acquisition and mastery of language and subsequent access to what Lacan has termed the 'three-dimensional register of the symbolic' – but they can still be subdued or partially socialised by a secondary web of restraining language. The psychiatrist therefore has not caught the truth of madness but has merely taught it to speak the same language back to him or her:

> As a result, a psychology of madness cannot be but derisory, and yet it touches on the essential. It is derisory because, in wishing to carry out a psychology of madness, one is demanding that psychology should undermine its own conditions, that it should turn back to that which made it possible, and that it should circumvent what is for it, by definition, the unsupersedable. *Psychology can never tell the truth because it is madness that holds the truth of psychology* ... If carried back to its roots, the psychology of madness would appear to be not the mastery of mental illness and hence the possibility of its disappearance, but the destruction of psychology itself and the discovery of that essential, nonpsychological because nonmoralisable relation that is the relation between Reason and Unreason.[6] [My italics]

It is at the junction of this relationship that we find the work of Deleuze and Guatarri. Opening up new and previously unexplored spaces of subjectivity, they offer the schizophrenic as the exemplary inhabitant of this penumbral area precariously balanced between reason and unreason – between the moralising tug of psychoanalysis and the implosive, inertial subject of postmodernism. In doing so they seek to expose an agenda that Foucault regarded as belonging as much to psychoanalysis and psychiatry as to other more embedded forms of 'rationalisation': 'What we call psychiatric practice is a certain moral tactic ... overlaid by myths of positivism.'[7]

It is this veil of positivism that shrouds psychoanalytic and psychiatric practice that is the subject of Deleuze and Guattari's critique. With its denunciation and exposure, they propose a radically new and Nietzschian conception of subjectivity and its attendant analysis.

What begins to emerge from the traditional and reified categorisations of psychopathological analysis is a conception of the schizophrenic as someone who is unable to suppress normal instincts to conform to an abnormal society. This is the Marcusian 'one-dimensional man' (sic) who realises his other dimensions only to be ostracised and marginalised in a society which adheres to the paradoxical notion of 'one-dimensional' individuality. The schizophrenic simply refuses to join in the chorus – in the united refrain 'we are all individuals'. But without the straitjacket of social conformity that underwrites the practices of psychoanalysis and psychiatry, identity itself becomes self-abolishing as it realises its dispersal through and across rather than 'in' the practices of its definition. This is the predicament that has faced the anti-psychiatric movement in general and Deleuze and Guattari in particular. (Note: Although I am using the terms antipsychiatric and anti-psychoanalytical in the broadest sense, it is worth noting that although the one may imply the other, they are not interchangeable.)

Although the forum of the 'anti-psychiatry' movement was the international review *Recherches*, which published articles chiefly from Italy (Basaglia, Jervis), England (Laing, Cooper), and France (Deleuze, Guattari), its apparent coherence as an international movement concealed profound divergences. In an interview in 1976 Guattari stated bluntly that, 'Today, one of the "inventors" of anti-psychiatry, Laing, is no longer connected with it: he says that he has never used the term. Basaglia believes it is a mystification that must be exposed. Meanwhile, in France, it has become something of a literary and cinematic genre.'[8] We might also add that in America there was no such movement at all, perhaps because there has never been a psychoanalytical orthodoxy to kick against. American 'psychoanalytical' practice has been and still is dispersed across a much wider range of activities and techniques – witnessed by the practices advertised in one San Francisco magazine[9] which range from primal scream and gestalt therapy to the 'multi-level healing' offered by the 'Platipus Ministry' entailing the 'harmonisation' of one's relationship to 'plants, animals, cars, xerox machines, sunsets, etc.' This hardly falls under the traditional Freudian umbrella. Nor can it be criticised (*pace* Foucault, Deleuze and Guattari) as just another round of whispering by the couch, since neither of these two 'psychoanalytical' components can be said to be present even given the most extended of metaphorical usages.

What is particular to Deleuze and Guattari's contribution to the antipsychiatry movement is that in attacking the specifically French institution that was initiated by Lacan, their critique takes on an anti-psychoanalytical dimension, never fully articulated in the work of their English counterparts Cooper and Laing. This must in part be due to the reestablishment and rehabilitation of Freudianism through Lacan into a new and greatly strengthened psychoanalytical orthodoxy – a process that again would have been much less discernible in England. Such a suggestion would seem to be supported by Guattari when he points to the fact that 'Lacanism isn't just a re-reading of Freud; it's something much more despotic, both as a theory and an institution, and far more rigid in its semiotic subjection of those who accept it.'[10]

Deleuze and Guattari: Oedipal reductionism

Unlike Lacan, Deleuze and Guattari define their position in opposition to Freud, condemning Lacan for accepting the assumptions of Oedipalism which they claim have permeated every aspect of psychoanalysis. In their most radical attack on the institution of Freudianism, *Anti-Oedipus: Capitalism and Schizophrenia*,[11] Deleuze and Guattari argue that psychoanalysis, in reducing everything to personalised, neuroticised, 'oedipalised' complexes of the unconscious, functions as an instrument of repression. Oedipalism in this context is the mode of symbolic interpretation which regresses all unconscious phenomena back to the primal family triangle – ironically referred to as the 'holy family' of 'mommy-daddy-me'. By such a method, analysis reduces the multiplicity of relations that an individual maintains with the social field to the single dimension represented by the Oedipus complex. The Oedipal fixation acts despotically: every psychic event comes to be interpreted as a covert manifestation of one underlying desire – incestuous sexual desire. Just as psychoanalysis tracks down the shifting moods and desires of the child, casting them practically from the womb (the stage at which the child is regarded as being polymorphously perverse) onto the rigid grid of adult sexuality, so the Oedipus complex functions within the psychoanalytical schema to provide a similar grid which 'fixes', stabilises and interprets adult desire by regressing it back to the child. It is a regress that is infinite in that it is self-perpetuating – each interpretation (adult and child) reflects as well as forms the other.

It is the pervasive Oedipalisation of desire that Deleuze and Guattari confront as the cornerstone of the psychoanalytical tyranny. Their claim is that 'the first error of psychoanalysis is in acting as if things began with the child'.[12] According to them, it is the paranoiac father who Oedipalises the son. Guilt therefore must be considered as an idea emanating from and projected by the father before it is an inner feeling experienced by the son.

> Oedipus is first the idea of an adult paranoiac, before it is the childhood feeling of a neurotic. So it is that psychoanalysis has much difficulty extracting itself from an infinite regression; the father must have been a child, but was able to be a child only in relation to a father, who himself was a child in relation to another father.[13]

The familial frame of reference functions as an absolute, thereby generating the appearance of a universalised and consequently de-politicised pysche. Whether the father works in a bank, goes off to a factory, is an immigrant labourer, is unemployed or is an alcoholic, he is 'Oedipalised' into becoming part of an undifferentiated social/familial machine. It is in this sense that Deleuze and Guattari argue that Oedipalism appears as a false attempt to reduce the unconscious to some single constant centre – the essential and original base that the postmodern account of the subject denies.

In taking into account the non-familial networks that also function in the construction of subjectivity, Deleuze and Guattari escape the reductivist view of the unconscious articulated in terms of an internalised constant, and instead view it as a productive sphere in direct contact with the outside world. The unconscious is no longer regarded as being individually generated out of private family experience, but socially generated out of collective public experience; 'Fantasy is never individual: it is group fantasy.'[14] The meanings of the unconscious are therefore on par with every other kind of meaning, and simulacrum of meaning, that spreads across society as a whole. Such meanings no more refer to individuals than they belong to individuals; 'the unconscious is utterly unaware of persons as such',[15] and does not recognise private ownership of utterance any more than of desire. The private mnemonic function of psychoanalysis gives way to the political analysis of public or collective fantasy. This is no longer hidden within the introverted recesses of the individual psyche but inscribed across the entire surface of the social body. Knowing oneself no longer entails delving within the oblivion of the unconscious mind for lost memories of painful (familial) experiences or unresolved conflicts: it now involves a rereading of those external and active (changing) public faces that Freudian analysis tended to dismiss as mere symptoms (manifestations) of an underlying (latent and also stable) psychic reality.

What it is claimed that the unconscious knows are social and political roles and public and historical events – 'all delirium possesses a world-historical, political and racial content.'[16] The topographical psychic network, against which psychoanalysis seeks to give form to individual subjectivity, is thus extended away from the privacy and stability of the familial base into the *political* domain of over-determined roles, stereotypes, flux and exchange: cops, robbers, Vietnam, *Apocalypse Now*, racial issues, economic crisis, defence systems, Star Wars, *Dallas*, *Neighbours*, TV stars, the media and so on. No longer conceived in terms of a hidden reality to be discovered through self-analysis, human nature is now redefined as the aggregate of the forms we have chosen to give public definitions of who we are.

What is lost in Deleuze and Guattari's anti-Oedipal formulation of the unconscious is the traditional reference points provided by Freud (and to a lesser extent Lacan) of the child and the primitive. Taking just childhood and the notion of regressive infantilism, it is easy to see how, in a postmodern culture that prioritises only the present, the stability that such a notion may once have provided now appears as simply another element in the legitimation of an institution which is in some discernible way enclosed and self-justifying. In order for childhood to remain the credible grounding component of a psychoanalytical theory, a margin or boundary must be established between the individual's present and past. But, as we have seen, postmodern culture integrates the past only by forcing it to disappear. Freud's insistence on the determining power of experience as a precedent for future behaviour belies a deep concern with origins. Present actions are always undertaken in the light of unconscious memories of the past. As the cultural demarcations between the past and the present become blurred, if not erased, and as past experiences become lost in the maze of formulas that we create to classify them, so self-understanding and analysis must be sought in the present. The re-politicisation of our understanding of the psyche therefore demands an inversion of the Freudian model of base and superstructure. Accordingly it is argued that we must now look towards the schizophrenic for our elucidation of the contemporary unconscious.

Schizoanalysis: rejecting binaries

With this inversion of orthodox psychoanalysis, in which the condition of the schizophrenic is seen as something to be cured, Deleuze and Guattari's proposed 'schizoanalysis' posits the schizophrenic as the 'Homo natura' from which psychoanalysis must take its bearings. In their own words, the aim of schizoanalysis is:

> To discover beneath the familial reduction the nature of the social in-vestments of the unconscious. To discover under the individual fantasy the nature of group fantasies. Or, what amounts to the same thing, to push the simulacrum to the point where it ceases to be an image of an image, so as to discover the abstract figures, the schizzes-flows that it harbours and conceals. To substitute, for the private subject of castra-tion, split into the subject of enunciation and the subject of the state-ment relating only to two orders of personal images, the collective agents of enunciation that for their part refer to mechanic arrangements. To overturn the theatre of representation into the order of desiring produc-tion: this is the whole task of schizoanalysis.[17]

The Lacanian account of schizophrenic experience in terms of the breakdown of the signifying chain seen primarily as a kind of communi-cation disorder, is, with Deleuze and Guattari, celebrated as a means of deterritorialising meanings that had appeared to be anchored to the repres-sive structures of capitalism. The schizophrenic lives the world as signs, as neither people nor things, but as endlessly proliferating meanings. S/he refuses to regress meanings back to 'origins' and instead reads the world as a discourse of surfaces – surfaces which intermingle, supersede and dis-place one another, but which never accumulate on a vertical axis. Mean-ings remain mobile and refuse to take their place within the order of things.

The schizophrenic's characteristic inability to hold his or her behaviour and state of mind together, under a conscious encompassing ego, leads to what has traditionally been pathologised under the terms 'split personality' and 'identification'. However, 'identification', according to Deleuze and Guattari, is actually an effect produced by the passage of meaning rather than any kind of personal identification, since, as is pointed out in the section entitled 'A Materialist Psychiatry', the schizophrenic often refuses to speak the word 'I', preferring to refer to him/herself as well as other people in the third person.[18] In refusing to enunciate the personal pronoun – the encompassing 'I' of experience – the schizophrenic refuses entry into what, as we have seen, Lacan termed the 'three-dimensional register of the symbolic'. Instead s/he remains exterior to him/herself, fascinated by the image or, in the extended sense used here, by the passage of meaning rather than its fixity within Lacan's three-dimensional schema constellated around the accession of language and the resolution of the Oedipus. The schizophrenic, like the subject of postmodernism, can therefore only situate the ego in the line of fiction.

This theorisation of identification as the passage of meaning corresponds to our everyday experience of advertisements, an experience of which Freud (and one sometimes suspects Lacan) can have had little knowledge. (There has always, according to Richard Harland, been a correspondence between the poststructuralists' way of theorising the world and the schizophrenics' way of living it.) Advertisements, where the chain of identification is intended to stretch from product to person/image to consumer – an example of which might be Chanel No. 5's use of Catherine Deneuve – operate not at the denotative level of the personal pronoun, but, as Barthes continually stressed, at the connotative level of culturally exchanged meaning. The consumer who 'identifies' with Catherine Deneuve is, according to the schizoanalysis proposed by Deleuze and Guattari, occupying much the same position within the flow and exchange of meaning as the traditionally defined schizophrenic who identifies with, for instance, Ghengis Khan – though of course their institutional status within society may well differ quite radically.

What is important about this rejection of the traditional and popular conception of 'identification' – seen as the movement between static, precreated and hermetic psychological entities and pathologised in terms of loss – is that it creates a theoretical space in which meaning can be regarded as simultaneously social and anti-social in such a way that it can be collapsed and subverted without resort to the intellectual's elitist claims to be exterior to it, or in some way exonerated from its rule.

The schizophrenic subversion of meaning is therefore celebrated in its capacity to overcome both the Oedipal determinations of the Freudian conception of subjectivity and the Lacanian notion of the subject as irrevocably bound to a social order that works in the service of repression. For the schizophrenic is never entirely taken over by the social institution of language which, according to Lacan, overtakes the child from the age of approximately 18 months. Meanings are both social and anti-social – social in the sense that the schizophrenic is open to public collective meanings and anti-social in his or her rejection of conventional codes and structures. This refusal to deal with social meanings as society would have them dealt with is the product of a refusal to observe boundaries between them. According to Deleuze and Guattari this apparently defective category formation and muddled thinking by association represents an alternative logic, a non-exclusive logic of 'either ... or ... or' in place of the old exclusive logic of 'either/or': 'Whereas the "either/or" claims to mark decisive choices between immutable terms (the alternative: either this or that), the schizophrenic "either ... or ... or" refers to the system of possible permutations between differences that always amount to the same as they shift and slide about.'[19] With this new logic, boundaries are only recognised in their transgression and meanings lose their differential encoded status as they are deterritorialised in the never-ending flux of their mutation. Thus the schizoid incapacity for concentrated and centred thinking is, in *Anti-Oedipus*, lauded as a revolutionary means of setting meaning in motion and multiplication in a way that corresponds to the poststructuralist reading of the text.

Postmodern/post-Oedipal subjectivity

One of the most significant paradoxes that Deleuze and Guattari tease out of their delirious analysis of contemporary subjectivity is the double-sidedness of its construction within the system of late capitalism. On the one hand, it is the uniquely rootless and restless nature of a postmodern society cast adrift from its old positivist moorings that conduces schizophrenic attitudes: 'everything in the system is insane: this is because the capitalist machine thrives on decoded and deterritorialised flows.'[20] What is being emphasised here is the degree to which late capitalist society resists the imposed structures that have characterised previous societies in its dependence on decoded flows of labour, production and capital. Simultaneously, however, there is an opposing movement towards a recoding, by which society represses the schizophrenic response to the 'schizz-flows' of the capitalist machine, thereby reimposing control. In their own words, 'what [civilised modern societies] deterritorialise with one hand, they re-territorialise with the other.'[21] Such reterritorialisations are seen to operate within the nuclear family and through the very structures of Oedipalisation which constitute the essence of the anti-psychoanalytical critique.

In exposing the way in which psychoanalysis operates imperially and in the service of capitalism, colonising subjectivity under Oedipal rule, Deleuze and Guattari attempt to show the way society uses these imposed structures in an attempt to obscure the consequences of its actual nature – more specifically how society uses psychoanalysis to teach us to desire our own repression. It is a society in which liberty now appears bilious and comic. In Baudrillard's words, we have come to realise that 'everyone secretly prefers an arbitrary and cruel order, which leaves him no choice, to the horrors of a liberal one in which he knows not what he wants and is forced to recognise that he knows not what he wants ...'[22] This vital dimension of choice can only be restored, according to Deleuze and Guattari, with entry into the pathologised realm of the schizophrenic.

What is being proposed, however, is not simply another theory of subjectivity to add to an already extensive repertoire. Rather, it is a non-neurotic form of politics which aims to determine new collective arrangements that can resist our totalitarian system of norms. This resistance, like the Baudrillardian conception of resistance as 'intensification of the same', acknowledges the pointlessness and futility of any desire to reverse the existing trends of capitalism. Instead it seeks to exacerbate the development of capitalism beyond Oedipalisation and into schizophrenisation, thereby creating a situation in which it can live out the consequences of its real nature.

For perhaps the flows are not yet deterritorialised enough, not decoded enough, from the viewpoint of a theory and a practice of a highly schizophrenic character. Not to withdraw from the process but to go further, to 'accelerate the process', as Nietzsche put it: in this matter, the truth is that we haven't seen anything yet.[23]

In attacking reductive psychoanalytical and political analyses *Anti-Oedipus* also attacks the internalisation, or what they would term the 'Oedipalisation' of desire, the capitalistic processes that neuroticise the self into desiring its own repression. They recognise that fascism is a problem that is neither national nor historical, but exists in everyone and every group whose 'superego' permits them to state, much like Nietzsche's man of resentment, that the other is evil (the Fascist, the Capitalist, the Communist), and hence that they themselves are good. The absolution of resentment encourages this desire to be led and to have someone else legislate one's life within the security of the herd. Reinforced by the psychoanalytical reduction of the self to the neuroticising core of Oedipus, such security reveals itself as no more than the desire to submit to the commonality – the silent majority. This is the fascism that causes every one of us to love power and to desire the very thing that dominates and exploits us. Quoting from Henry Miller's *Sexus*, Mark Seem indicates the hopelessness of thinking in these terms: ' "The man who looks for security, even in the mind, is like the man who would chop off his limbs in order to have artificial ones that will give him no pain and trouble." (p. 428) No pain, no trouble – this is the neurotic's dream of a tranquilised and conflict-free existence.'[24]

Within the curious ambivalence of a society which decentres ('deterritorialises') only to reinscribe desire within its own prescriptive terms, neurosis appears not as an illness but as a paradoxical form of normality. Society maintains the individual on the verge of breakdown, merchandising the 'protection' offered by the psychoanalytical model in exchange for submission. As Lotringer points out in relation to sexual perversion – a context that can be extended to include the psychic 'abnormality' of neurosis in general: 'If as Freud asserted, perverse tendencies are present in everyone, then perverts far from being helpless maniacs or hopeless degenerates may be considered "successful neurotics" ... Perversion is the negative side of neurosis, since it succeeds in implementing the desires that keep lurching at the threshold of inhibited consciousness.'[25] By the same reasoning, the schizophrenic might be regarded as a 'successful capitalist' since s/he lives the reality of a system based on deterritorialisation and flux. He or she lives psychotically, as it were, on the very threshold of meaning.

Like their English (anti-psychiatric) counterparts, Cooper and Laing, Deleuze and Guattari suggest that the psychotic and the schizophrenic may possess a superior truth to the constantly Oedipalised neurotic. Both fight against the pathologisation of ego-loss that is the impediment to a collective non-fascist politics of healing. Both look to the psychotic and the schizophrenic in a paradoxical attempt to cure us of the cure itself, since they are incapable of being Oedipalised, even and especially by psychoanalysis, as it is only the neurotic who seeks to transform every desire into discourse. However, despite this, the texts read very differently. The common rejection of schizophrenia as a psychiatric model along with an emphatic agreement that the therapist who consents to such a classification becomes part of the problem rather than the solution, disguises the fact that Laing's work is primarily a critique of the institution of psychiatry and the reductive grounding of its diagnostic methods. But, the collaboration between Guattari the psychiatrist/militant and Deleuze the philosopher has produced something different. For although, as Foucault points out in the preface, *Anti-Oedipus* is not a flashy Hegel and refuses to be read as the new theory or philosophy of the subject, as a critique, it does extend to include all those Oedipalising processes that delineate the bounds, the construction and the institution of subjectivity itself. In doing so it presents a revolutionary politics of desire, a non-neurotic politics freed by the schizophrenic from the Oedipal yoke of capitalism.

How does this relate to postmodernism and in particular Frederic Jameson's articulation of schizophrenia as a new and in some way appropriately postmodern 'aesthetic model'? To recall Jameson's argument, the schizophrenic's way of experiencing the world in terms of the literal signifier in isolation, corresponds to the postmodern breakdown of temporality and what he terms the waning of affect. This he laments as it signals the end of the depth model of expression which is predicated on a conception of the subject as monadic – as a kind of receptacle capable of ordering and cataloguing experience according to its own internal structures. It also entails the collapse of meaningful distinctions between the authentic and the inauthentic. However, when Jameson evokes Lacan's account of schizophrenic experience, seen in terms of the breakdown of the signifying chain, he does so in order to elucidate a spatial model of the psyche that could correspond to what he terms 'the new spatial logic of the simulacrum'. Undoubtedly there is such a reading of Lacan, but given that Jameson is attempting to restore some notion of authenticity to the depthlessness of the postmodern subject, the work of Deleuze and Guattari would have provided a much more appropriate departure point. What they celebrate is the schizophrenic's creative and revolutionary capacity to resist the encoded flows of desire. The subjectivity that they imply, though never formulate, is both spatial, operating across rather than through the capitalist body, and authentic, in that it is non-neurotic, thus proposing a politics of the self that escapes Oedipalisation.

By placing the emphasis on desire rather than experience, Deleuze and Guattari allow the schizophrenic a scene in which determinate agency is, to a certain extent, restored. In contrast, Baudrillard uses the schizoid as metaphor of contemporary existence, in a way that leaves no room for negotiation, no scene, only the (ob)scene screen that is the desert of the real. This is a radically formulated account of depthless experience, in which all interiority is forced into extroversion. And, like Deleuze and Guattari, he draws on the old metaphors of psychopathology to describe the irreversible loss of the sovereignty of the symbolic space that was that of the subject:

> If hysteria was the pathology of the exacerbated staging of the subject, a pathology of expression, of the body's theatrical and operatic conversion: and if paranoia was the pathology of organisation, of the structuration of a rigid and jealous world: then with communication and information, with the immanent promiscuity of all these networks, with their continual connections, we are now in a new form of schizophrenia. No more hysteria, no more projective paranoia, properly speaking, but this state of terror proper to the schizophrenic; too greater proximity of everything which touches, invests and penetrates without resistance, with no halo of private protection, not even his own body, to protect him anymore.
>
> The schizo is bereft of every scene, open to everything inspite himself, living in the greatest confusion. He is himself obscene, the obscene prey of the world's obscenity. What characterises him is less the loss of the real, the light years of estrangement from the real, the pathos of distance and radical separation as is commonly said: but very much the contrary, the absolute proximity, the total instantaneity of things, the feeling of no defense, no retreat. It is the end of interiority and intimacy, the overexposure and transparence of the world which traverses him without obstacle. He can no longer produce the limits of his own being, can no longer play nor stage himself, can no longer produce himself as mirror. He is now only a pure screen, a switching centre for all the networks of influence.[26]

This 'pure screen' of subjectivity is for Baudrillard the site of infinite implosion. Strategic resistance, which was once the liberating claim of subjecthood, is now reduced to the status of myth. All reference disappears as imperialist expansion finally reverses its direction and attacks itself. Even Deleuze and Guattari's rhizomatic analysis submits to this expansionist logic. According to Baudrillard, the reference of desire that was born in psychoanalysis merely achieves maturity in the form of shattered molecular desire in the anti-psychoanalytical arguments of *Anti-Oedipus*. In this sense, they still belong to the final phase of imperialism and the great ideology of liberation. This is the very ideology that is rejected by Baudrillard and to which we shall return in the concluding chapter.

Notes

1 R.D. Laing, *The Divided Self* (Pelican, 1965) p.36.
2 See Sylvère Lotringer's *Overexposed: Treating Sexual Perversion in America* (Autonomedia, 1988).
3 See François Meltzer (ed.), *The Trial(s) of Psychoanalysis* (University of Chicago Press, 1987).
4 Joseph Berke quoted in Felix Guattari's *Molecular Revolution: Psychiatry and Politics* (Peregrine, 1984) p.56.
5 Laing, *The Divided Self*, p.20.
6 Michel Foucault, *Mental Illness and Psychology* (University of California Press, 1987) p.74.
7 Foucault, *Madness and Civilisation: A History of Insanity in the Age of Reason* (Tavistock, 1967) p.276.
8 Guattari, *Molecular Revolution*, p.44.
9 Drawn from *Common Ground – Resources for Personal Transformation* (Fall 1986).
10 Guattari, *Molecular Revolution*, p.49.
11 Deleuze and Guattari, *Anti-Oedipus: Capitalism and Schizophrenia* (Viking Press, 1977).
12 Ibid., p. 275.
13 Ibid., p. 274.
14 Ibid., p. 30.
15 Ibid., p. 46.
16 Ibid., p. 88.
17 Ibid., p. 271.
18 Ibid., p. 23.
19 Ibid., p. 12.
20 Ibid., p. 347.
21 Ibid., p. 257.
22 Jean Baudrillard, *Les Strategies Fatales* (Paris, 1983) p. 241 – translated extract appearing in Mark Poster (ed.), *Jean Baudrillard: Selected Writings* (Polity Press, 1988).
23 Deleuze and Guattari, *Anti-Oedipus*, pp.239–40.

24 Quoted in introduction to *Anti-Oedipus*.
25 Lotringer, *Overexposed*, p.13.
26 Baudrillard, 'The Ecstasy of Communication' in Hal Foster (ed.), *Postmodern Culture* (Pluto Press, 1985) pp.132–3.

7 Space on Flat Earth: Disney

History? I don't have the slightest notion of it.
Donald Duck in a library

History is hysterical: it is constituted only if we consider it, only if we look at it – and in order to look at it we must be excluded from it ...
Roland Barthes, *Camera Lucinda*

Introduction: Two views of the second world

In an article entitled 'The Bottom Line on Planet One',[1] Dick Hebdige asks the reader to imagine a galaxy containing two quite different worlds. The worlds that he describes are separated by an unbridgeable gulf that corresponds roughly to the sort of schism that separates the modern from the postmodern. In the first world, 'the relations of power and knowledge are so ordered that priority and precedence are given to written and spoken language over "mere (idolatrous) imagery." '[2] This is a world that is understood hermenuetically, in which meaning is excavated from underneath dissembling appearances and consigned and indexed to the stockpile of knowledge that constitutes our self-understanding – our history. Access to this body of knowledge is limited to the few, and requires long, arduous and often expensive rites of initiation. In contrast, the second world is infinitely more democratic. Access to this world is gained primarily through the medium of the image rather than the word. It is a world which is directly apprehensible since its truths are not closeted in the barely penetrable vaults that hold real insight, but rather these second world truths are, if they exist at all, inscribed on the very surface of our images and being. Here everything is immanent, as the past and future coalesce in the eternal present, the here and now of the image. 'Because there is no history, there is no contradiction – just random conjunctions of semantic particles (images and words).'[3]

This second world is the 'Babel 17' of postmodernity. As in Samuel R. Delany's classic science fiction novel[4] the new 'language' – here the flat, uninflected 'second world' language of the image – initiates a wholly new range of epistemological possibility, having severed its ties to the first world systems of *structural* linguistics and relations of power and knowledge. It is to be distinguished from the older language, which it contests by the absence of any personal pronouns. The user is therefore ego-less and unable to unify experience within the hermeneutical circle in time that allows the past and projected future to inform and determine the present. Those who can use the language necessarily adopt the characteristics of the schizophrenic, the experience of the signifier in its pure material form that precludes either moral inflection or critical distance. The narrative of the novel pivots around this crucial difference of semantic im/possibility. But, although the struggle appears to take the binary and oppositional form represented by the two language systems, what it actually confronts is not the nature of the ascendancy or merit of one system over another, but rather the omnipotence and seduction of a system that is beyond the relative assignation of value – in Nietzsche's phrase, beyond good and evil.

To invoke such a system is to move outside the rationalist theology of representation. It cannot be described but only provoked, in the sense used by Baudrillard when he claims that his primary concern is not the negation of the real, but rather the issuing of a challenge. It therefore comes as no surprise that his later work should have much more in common with science fiction than with conventional theoretical discourse. Baudrillard's prominence as the exemplary strategist of the second world is as the al-chemist of the real, who, like the science fiction writer, casts radical doubt upon the first world by continually transmuting its claims to reality into flat second world images; its languages into Delany's babel. The 'reality' which we clutch, grasp, reinvent and ultimately reconstitute and rediss-eminate in this second world, now reappears in the form of its sanitised and peculiarly precious reincarnation – as an absolute and inviolable utopia.

Before returning to Baudrillard's own 'theoretical' wanderings through and around these territories, we must take a detour into the actual (non)space in which the second world subject moves, dissolves and re-appears. It is a detour which leads us initially through the non-space of Disney World – the illustrious grazing ground and meeting place of first world infidels and second world high-priests, gurus and acolytes. Here we can indulge in a sort of amnesic intoxication, born of the triumph of forgetting over memory and of effect over cause. In celebrating the 'liber-ation' of both the subject and the referent from their previous entangle-ment within stultifying 'first world' dialectics – of truth and falsity, inside and outside, reality and imagination – we find ourselves 'cruising' a utopian postmodern space which answers only to the depthless logic of the consumer/leisure industry. Juxtaposing this view of second world hyper-reality we find the dystopian space portrayed in the film *Blade Runner*. It is the space of struggle, a site of contestation, radically different though no less postmodern than the one we have left behind. It is, to paraphrase Barthes, a multidimensional space in which a variety of texts, none of them original, blend. What distinguishes them from the second world of Disney, however, is that they also clash . . .

Disney: utopian postmodernism

Perhaps the greatest monument to the 'second world' depthless aesthetics of hyperreality lies in the 'realised' kingdom of the imaginary created by Walt Disney. His achievements testify precisely to Baudrillard's by now familiar theorisation of a culture that prefers the copy to the original and for which 'The very definition of the real has become that which it is possible to give an equivalent reproduction ... The real is not only that which can be reproduced, but that which is already reproduced ... The hyperreal ... which is entirely simulation.'[5] In setting out to realise the American dream, Disney's success can only be understood in terms of a desire to fabricate an imaginative reality which in the Baudrillardian sense could outstrip and outbid the 'external' reality against which its claims to the imaginary have usually been judged. The hyperreality of Disney is in this sense 'more real than real'.

The significance of Disney's particular achievements and what might be termed the pervasive 'disneyfication' of postmodern culture generally, derives from the way in which it problematises fundamental notions regarding the authenticity of cultural experience – experience which, in a Disney World, is no longer tethered to any conception of an external, pre-ordained or immutable reality. Instead it is manufactured by exactly the sort of 'culture *industry*' that caused so much consternation amongst the denizens of Frankfurt (Adorno, Horkheimer, Marcuse *et al.*), whose distaste for 'popular' or 'mass' culture in the US was perhaps, as one critic put it, because they saw it as 'a more developed if less sinister form of the hysterical "rationalisation" pursuing its "final solution" in their native Germany'.[6]

What was inherited from them was a view of American mass culture as manipulation – as a process of degrading, dehistoricising and defiling 'real' human needs by providing them only with 'false', 'disneyfied' solutions. With hindsight we can more easily see the irony lurking in both the vitriol and the concern of their critique. Namely that the culture being denounced from the 'olympian' heights of Eurocentricism denies such denunciations by blurring the boundaries between artifice and reality, 'real' and 'false' needs upon which their critique was based. The cultural 'other' of European 'high art' (for the Frankfurt refugees), against which claims to authenticity had traditionally been put to the test, has been lost as the stability of the paired oppositions upon which it had been based is called into question. The disappearance of aesthetics and higher values in kitsch and hyperreality, like the disappearance of history and the real in the televisual, refuses to assume the mask of tragedy or adopt the pathos of loss – instead it invokes a sort of abject fascination with the mechanisms of disappearance and absolute indifference. Hyperreality, in refusing to distinguish between manufactured (degraded) and natural (authentic) experience, therefore denies us the luxury of the old-fashioned ideological critique, couched as it was between the terms of misrepresentation and falsification. In the case of the Disney consumer, who is being misrepresented and what is being falsified?

The coordinates of value that had served to elevate the critique above its subject seem to have imploded in our age of hyperreality: as the subject itself, in this case the whole of American society, has become dispersed in, and ultimately indistinguishable from, its various representations. To attempt to claim that Disney somehow exists apart from this orbit of representation is clearly untenable. No amount of disdain can disguise our complicity in the promulgation of the Disney experience, and the anatomy of pleasure that it exposes, even when it adopts the inverted, derisive form posited by the cultural elite. What this chapter seeks to reject are the antonymical oppositions of real and imaginary, truth and falsity that sustain the imperial dismissal of whole areas of culture as being in some way self-evidently inauthentic. The aim, however, is not one of rehabilitation, but rather a re-examination of Disney as, in certain ways, apotheosising and celebrating the various processes of collapse that render this sort of binarism obsolete.

Dorfman and Mattelart's *How to Read Donald Duck*[7] is perhaps the most significant of traditional ideological analyses, and undoubtedly the most notorious. Banned in Chile after the September 1983 coup and in the United States in 1975, the book sets out to examine the imperialist ideology contained within the Disney cartoon text. The analysis provided by Dorfman and Mattelart penetrates the apparent innocence of the world inhabited by Donald Duck and his various relations, to reveal the 'real' political economy that underlies it. The duck world of the comics offers a 'utopian' vision that in many ways corresponds structurally to the diagnosis of contemporary society provided by fearful postmodernists. The constitutive features of postmodernity described by Frederic Jameson;[8] the waning of affect; the rise of aesthetic populism; the globalisation of culture and most significantly the loss of history, are all in varying degrees evident in the duck society that is Disney's creation. It is the utopian vision/version of a world from which all the depth models that account for the inherent tensions of modernism have been banished in the face of a seamless synchronicity. In Disney, the characters provide perfect profiles of the various surfaces that intermingle in the postmodern problematic. Three-dimensional (human) social life, with its complexity of relations, interactions and meanings, is here safely re-presented as two-dimensional pond life.

In a chapter entitled, 'Uncle, Buy Me a Contraceptive . . .' Dorfman and Mattelart approach the absented historical dimension of Disney society by examining and tracing the genealogy of its various inhabitants. The first and most striking observation to be made is the curious absence of parentage:

> Disney's is a universe of uncles and grand-uncles, nephews and cousins: the male-female relationship is that of eternal fiances. Scrooge McDuck is Donald's uncle, Grandma Duck is Donald's aunt (but not Scrooge's

wife), and Donald is the uncle of Huey, Dewey and Louie. Cousin Gladstone Gander is a 'distant nephew' of Scrooge; he has a nephew of his own called Shamrock ...[9]

Clearly this is a predominantly masculine society, composed as it is of bachelors and nephews. Matrimonial bonds have been discarded in favour of the avuncular relationship which bypasses those problems of loyalty, genesis and affection that seem to afflict only those with parentage. Oedipal development, normally understood to be a constitutive part of adult psychology, is omitted, as are the dirty, often complicated and not always successful processes of sexual procreation. But in being spared the archaic hassle of being born, the ducks and related Disney characters are also committed to life in a social orphanage that prohibits differentiation according to those factors that, taken as a whole, form the rubric of personal history. This is reiterated by Dorfman and Mattelart when they point out that the characters

> only function by virtue of a suppression of real and concrete factors; that is their personal history, their birth and death, and their whole development in between, as they grow and change. Since they are not engendered by any biological act, Disney characters may aspire to immortality: whatever apparent, momentary sufferings are inflicted on them in the course of their adventures, they have been liberated, at least, from the curse of the body.[10]

With any future demographic increases being attributable only to extra-sexual factors, the duplication of characters as twins and triplets comes as no surprise. Donald's nephews, Daisy's nieces, the Beagle boys and the piglets are all triplets, whilst the chipmunks, mice and the nephews of Woody Woodpecker, to name but a few, are all twins. Such a proliferation of twins and triplets suggests an interesting preoccupation with cloning as the form of non-sexual genesis. With no sexual reproduction liable to shuffle the genetic cards, diversity amongst the ducks is guarded against and proliferation appears to be viral rather than biological. But when viewed allegorically, the Disney twins and triplets no longer belong only to the realm of a distant and unrealised future. For as Baudrillard has pointed out, cloning has now become an immediate reality of genetic engineering by which the process of reproduction has become detached from the sexual act.[11] However, the cloning process is not confined to the genesis of various cartoon characters. It applies metaphorically to the whole Disney project of 'imagineering' and represents a new relationship to the mirror of the 'other'.

In a short story published in *The Book of Sand*',[12] Jorges Luis Borges raises the issue of cloning in a descriptive passage in which the wandering self confronts its double. In the ensuing examination of the doubling character of narrative and mediation, the encounter with his doppelganger, 'the other', is explained in terms of the other person's capacity to dream the real – concluding in the end that 'the other man dreamed me.' Exploiting indirectly the familiar Biblical injunction against graven images and more directly the horror of exact replication and the duplication of narrative, the Borgesian tale attempts to confront the nature of a world, like the world created by Disney, in which appearances have become things in themselves. With the loss of the guarantee of the other, we lose the promise of delayed and annulled self-confrontation. Unlike the double, doppelganger or 'other', which enacts a romantic reaffirmation of the grounded self, the clone asserts a higher reality – to use the Baudrillardian phrase it is 'more real than real'. In describing the threatening loss of space between reality and the mediated world of appearances, Borges leaves us only with the vision of a flat world in which the space of differentiation that is our history has been all but erased.

This Borgesian world parallels that inhabited by our Disney friends. It is a utopian world in which the past exists and is known only through the present. In this sense history is conceived as a process of synchronic repetition in which memory and the interrelated chains of knowledge that constitute our historical identity have been lost and the world is understood only as a ceaseless prefiguration of the Disney present. The mirror of the historical 'other' in which the present has traditionally tested its representations is no longer capable of restoring the temporal dimension to this society in which both the past and the future have become colonised by the structures of the present. The result is a peculiar utopia – an orphanage conditioned by the genesis of its inmates. Never having been born, the Disney characters can never grow up. In short, they aspire to immortality, an aspiration echoed in the cryogenisation of their creator.

At an allegorical level, the world of Disney represents a loss of temporality that corresponds precisely with recent formulations of the postmodern condition. But whereas Disney celebrates liberation from the yoke of the past and the inertial weight of history, postmodern theorists such as Jameson have articulated the same position in terms only of loss, and of the emergence of a new and depthless type of subjectivity. Although Jameson chooses schizophrenics as examples of this type of subjectivity, Walt's happy ducks would have been just as good. For, in Dorfman and Mattelart's words, 'By eliminating a character's effective past, and at the same time denying him the opportunity of self-examination in relation to his present predicament, Disney denies him the only perspective from which he can look at himself, other than from the world in which he has always been submerged.'[13] In lacking the temporal unification of the past and future through the experience of the present, the Disney characters described by Dorfman and Mattelart correspond closely to the 'schizophrenics' described by Jameson. The predicative conditions would appear to be the same, both involving a failure 'to unify the past, present and future of our own biographical experience of psychic life'.[14] (Fortunately, in neither case is the consequence of this failure too dire – Jameson, like the ducks, seems happy to represent the 'schizophrenic' loss of temporality in terms of the dissolution of anxiety and its sublimation in a jolly rain of orgasmic and unrelated instants draped in a sort of hallucinogenic hilarity . . .)

However, to say that if Donald Duck had an adult psyche he would by necessity be a schizophrenic, hardly advances any understanding of our relationship to a 'Disney' (postmodern) culture. What these observations do indicate is the relative positions of Dorfman/Mattelart's and Jameson's critiques. 'The Cultural Logic of Late Capitalism', from which the quotation by Jameson is taken, is primarily a diagnostic account of a contemporary condition – though as we have seen in Chapter 4 it is not uninflected. In contrast the work of Dorfman and Mattelart presents itself as a direct critique of the Disney institution. In this sense it belongs to the tradition based on readings of the early work of Louis Althusser, which provides the basis for ideological criticism, according to which ideology is seen to represent 'the imaginary relationship of individuals to their real conditions of existence'.[15] In arguing that Disney characters function only by virtue of the suppression of the 'real' and concrete factors of personal history, birth, death and the development in between, their critique falls directly within that very well-defined nexus of debate that circulates around issues of authenticity.

Given the correspondences between the Dorfman/Mattelart analysis of duck society and Jameson's account of contemporary psychic life, both of which point to a radical loss of any sense of history or of the past as being capable of granting coherence to present existence, we might well ask what it is that distinguishes the two approaches. The difference lies in the way in which the notion of authenticity is interrogated. For Jameson the 'other' of postmodernism, represented by this new type of depthless experience, has become a general cultural condition to the extent that it can no longer even be constituted as 'the other', except by reactionary ideologues wishing to resurrect and reclaim a now mythical past, in a vain attempt to stave off the incursions of the present. In other words, the schizophrenic who epito-mises this condition, has now been reformulated as the 'homo natura' of postmodernity. The 'authentic', if it still makes sense to use the term, has effectively shifted its ground. However, it has done so in a way that is self-abolishing, since the concept of authenticity itself makes little sense without invoking the 'depth models' that have hitherto attended it.

In contrast, Dorfman and Mattelart presuppose a stable notion of what constitutes authentic experience, and by extension culture. The world of Walt Disney fails to fall into this category for two reasons. First, it resists interpretation according to depth models whose function is to restore meaning under the dissimulating facade of appearances: secondly, and perhaps the greater heresy, is that it represents an imaginary (and by implication falsified) set of relations to our real conditions of existence. However, the problem with such a denunciation is that it presupposes a reality that is external, immutable and independent of its various representations – presuppositions against which we have been more than adequately cautioned by writers such as Baudrillard. The 'real' conditions of existence that Dorfman and Mattelart attempt to excavate from their 'disneyfied' perversions are, in fact, conditions that no longer pertain to the Disney culture that is supposedly the subject of their analysis. Given this, their work must be viewed as a nostalgic attempt to recover and restore a set of relations that are appropriate only to a pre-Disney era – a paradise lost of ideology.

What is missed, which is so fundamental to the Disney experience, is that it belongs to an era of simulation that no longer corresponds to the ideological period that it has superseded. In Baudrillard's words, whereas 'ideology corresponds to the betrayal of reality by signs: simulation corresponds to the short-circuit of reality and its reduplication by signs. It is always the aim of ideological analysis to restore the objective process: it is always a false problem to want to restore the truth beneath the simulacrum.'[16] Such underlying truths are no longer available in the hyper-visible world of Disney: it conceals nothing under the promiscuity and ubiquity of its imagery. With this fatal shortcircuiting of reality and the image, all systems of meaning become confounded. Ideology as a means of mapping the intersections between the 'real' and the 'imaginary' loses any effectivity as a critical 'tool'. Having shed even the *illusion* of its former powers of discrimination, ideology can now reappear only as an empty simulacrum.

By 1966, only one decade into the profit-making era, Walt Disney Productions estimated that around the world 240,000,000 people had seen a Disney movie, 100,000,000 had watched a Disney television show every week, 800,000,000 had read a Disney book or magazine, 50,000,000 had listened or danced to Disney music or records, 80,000,000 had bought Disney-licensed merchandise, 150,000,000 had read a Disney comic strip and 80,000,000, had seen Disney educational films at school, at work or in church.[17] However, despite the enormity of these figures, it has, since Disney's death in December 1966, been the theme parks rather than the movies, publications and merchandise that have funded the Disney operation. Now more than 33 years old, the original 'Disneyland' theme park has spawned a number of relations: 'Walt Disney World' in Orlando, Florida; 'EPCOT' (Experimental Prototype Community of Tomorrow) at the same location; Tokyo's Disneyland built under franchise (Oriental Land Company); and most recently 'Eurodisney', still in the early stages of development. It is in the theme parks that we find the most complete 'realisation' of Disney's American dream, which apotheosises the nature of what has been described as 'this most unnatural of all utopias'.[18]

Making their debut in 1955 with the opening of Disneyland, the theme parks represent a continuation of Disney's obsession with the creation, simulation and reanimation of life, though on a scale quite unprecedented within the cartoon world. Partially funded by the ABC television network, for whom Disney provided a weekly, hour-long slot, the Disneyland project benefited from having both a promotional outlet and a pilot scheme. The other great advantage of the ABC contract was that Disneyland was seen to be continuous with the earlier film and animation projects, from which Disney had earned his reputation as the Midas of the child's imagination. It was thus presented as the *Gesamtkunstwerk* of contemporary American culture, combining history, imagination and of course fun. The project, once formulated, was defined in the following way:

> The idea of Disneyland is a simple one. It will be a place for people to find happiness and knowledge.
>
> It will be a place for parents and children to share pleasant times in one another's company: a place for teachers and pupils to discover greater ways of understanding and education. Here the older generation can recapture the nostalgia of days gone by, and the younger generation can savour the challenge of the future. Here will be the wonders of Nature and Man for all to see and understand.
>
> Disneyland will be based upon and dedicated to the ideals, the dreams and hard facts that have created America. And it will be uniquely equipped to dramatise these dreams and facts and to send them forth as a source of courage and inspiration to all the world.
>
> Disneyland will be something of a fair, an exhibition, a playground, a community center, a museum of living facts, and a showpiece of beauty and magic.
>
> It will be filled with the accomplishments, the joys and hopes of the world we live in. And it will remind us how to make those wonders part of our own lives.[19]

Reading like a utopian manifesto, this outline of the Disneyland project provides us with an insight into an understanding of Disney's previous film work which must be regarded as a blueprint for the later theme parks. The films fall into two categories. The first, of which *Snow White* (1937) or *Sleeping Beauty* (1959) are classic examples, are tales of death, rebirth, suspended animation and miraculous redemption. These themes find their corollary in the Disneyland experience. The past, as we shall see, is represented as a dead and inert mass, committing the future to an unwanted half-life that can only be broken when it is coopted by the imagination of the child and resurrected in the present. Whilst history is resurrected from the dead only to be reborn within the theme parks, the visitors themselves are required to suspend animation when they enter the mecca of fun; to leave one's car is in a sense to leave something of one's American humanity and in an act of abandonment to consign oneself to another power. Restoration and redemption occur only when one returns to the parking lot and re-enters the 'reality' of the non-Disney world, bearing, and enhanced by, the fruit of the Disney experience. Walt's reality redeems American reality within this spiralling and tautologous logic of the 'second world'.

The second and perhaps more familiar Disney theme involves the grafting of real actors into imaginary landscapes. *Alice in Cartoonland* (1922), *Alice in Wonderland* (1951), *Mary Poppins* (1964), *Tron* (1982) and even the relatively recent production, *Down and Out in Beverly Hills*, can all be read as in some way exploring the genre established by Lewis Caroll. However, it is in the theme parks that we see the soliloquy to this Carollian obsession – where 'real' people meet the 'reality' of their childhood dreams. In this un(adult)erated utopia, the epiphany of the hyperreal pervades not just the spectacle, but also the whole set of relations that participate in its existence. As Debord was to claim in the late 1960s, 'The spectacle is not just a collection of images, but a social relation among people mediated by images.'[20] It is as models of social organisation that relinquish the necessity of a grounding reality principle that Disneyland, and the later parks, most notably EPCOT, reveal their most utopian ambitions and aspirations.

Despite the fact that the theme parks cater primarily for adults, who outnumber children by four to one, it is the imagination of the child that is conceived as the past and future utopia of the adult. The child is seen to represent a state of nature forfeited by the complexity of adult life. The omnipresence of animals within the Disney world also helps to reinforce the suggestion that it is nature itself that pervades and determines the whole complex of social relations. In situations where the 'natural' surrogates for the innocence of the childish imagination no longer seem appropriate, as in the inescapably acculturated climate of 'Main Street', regression is induced by diminution. Disney explains the miniaturisation of the architecture in the following terms: 'We had every brick, shingle and gas lamp made five-eighths true size. This costs more, but made the street a toy, and the imagination can play more freely with a toy. Besides, people like to think that their world is somehow more grown-up than Papa's was.'[21] Undoubtedly part of the success of the Disney enterprise can be attributed to this subtle ability to colonise not just a particular sphere of entertainment, but the whole of reality with the analgesic of the child's imagination.

In successfully reterritorialising the imaginary within the benign and dehistoricised circumference of preadolescent childhood, Disney writes a history that is answerable only to the pantheon of fun. In Disney world, time is apprehended as a consumable entity, and history becomes a marketplace in which whole cultures and civilisations are valued according to the plebiscite of purchase. In EPCOT, for instance, the World Showcase comprises ten small nations situated around an artificial lake. As Paul Taylor points out, 'a panning gaze across the horizon can take in everything from the Eiffel Tower to a pagoda to the Piazza San Marco. It's the epitome of modern tourism, representing, in Guy Debord's words, "the leisure of visiting what has become banal".'[22] It is a place of absolute iconism, each country depicted becoming coextensive with its representation. Here the simulacra, the copy for which there is no original, reigns supreme. The England of the pub, Twinings and tobacco, like the Germany of continual 'Oktoberfest', become more real than real in their consumable representations. As allegories of consumer capitalism, the Disney theme parks illustrate an era in which cultural (or for that matter personal) identity, once dispersed in representation, can only be reconstructed through the privileged act of consumption itself. In the Disney parks, the reality of trade is blended with the play of fiction so that the customer finds him or herself participating in the 'fantasy' because of his/her own authenticity as a consumer. It is exactly this erasure of the distinction between historical reality and fantasy that makes theatricality explicit to the point at which Eco claims that, 'the hallucination operates in making the visitors take part in the scene and thus become participants in that commercial fair that is apparently an element in the whole fiction but in fact represents the substantial aim of the whole imitative machine'.[23]

The transformation of the image into consumer spectacle recalls the Situationist analysis. Remembering Debord's description of a society in which 'The image has become the final form of commodity reification ... the spectacle is capital to such a degree that it becomes the image',[24] we find in Disney World only the lobotomised blandness of the insipid spectacle, the domesticated sign of an artificial paradise. Always privileging the visual over the bodily, the theme parks are in a sense the apotheosis of a drive-in culture. It is a culture that caters for the post-urban being described by Eco, for a new type of person who '... considers his right foot a limb designed for pressing the accelerator, and the left an atrophied appendix, because cars no longer have a clutch – eyes are something to focus, at a steady driving speed, on visual-mechanical wonders, signs, constructions that must impress the mind in the space of a few seconds'.[25] In this environment, it has made sense to substitute the kinaesthetic attraction of traditional amusements – the 'flea-bitten',[26] white-knuckle rides of Coney Island – with the sanitised enjoyment of a 360-degree projection around a static audience. The profusion of gadgetry necessary to facilitate these processes and effects makes the place redolent not of a funfair but rather of a hospital intensive care ward – prepared and waiting to incubate the experientially deprived. The absolute privileging of the gaze denies the body and the mortality of the flesh. Consequently, in Paul Taylor's words, the publicists can, proudly describe EPCOT as the best equipped city on earth for the handicapped, which only means, however that it is as dynamically demanding as a hospital corridor ... Freedom of movement is purely illusory: the visitor is trapped in the spectacle's theatricality. In Disneyland critic Louis Marin claims, 'the visitor is on the stage; he performs the play and is alienated from the part without being aware of performing.' But the French critic missed a crucial point during his American vacation. What he calls alienation is here called great fun.[27]

As the quintessence of consumer ideology, the Disney parks offer a continual incitement to consumption that is obscured by a belief in play and, by extension, in having fun. It is a form of fun that is derived entirely from the play of illusions and phantasms. The flat surface of consumption that is the distinguishing feature of our postmodern culture holds no secrets since nothing is hidden and the subterfuge of the oppositional dialectic has imploded, leaving only the single dimension of a totality. In this world, as Arnold Hauser puts it,

The dream becomes the paradigm of the whole world-picture, in which reality and unreality, logic and fantasy, the banality and sublimation of existence, form an indissoluble and inexplicable unity ... Art is siezed by a real mania for totality. It seems possible to bring everything into relationship with everything else, everything seems to include itself within the law of the whole ... the accent is now on the simultaneity of the contents of consciousness, the immanence of the past in the present, the constant flowing together of different periods of time ... the impossibility of defining the media in which the mind moves.[28]

The media in which Disney's mind moved was that of the dream. Like the surrealists, he regarded dreaming as an inspired state, in the double sense of the word. As an existing condition or state of mind, the Disney dream was also envisaged as an organised political community. When asked about the nature of this dream, Disney reputedly used to quote Archibald Macleish, claiming that, 'there are those, I know, who will reply that the liberation of humanity, the freedom of man and the mind, is nothing but a dream ... they are right, it is an American dream.'[29]

The attraction and fascination of the Disney theme parks, therefore lies not in the evanescence of illusion and fantasy, but the pervasive 'reality' of the American dream as it has penetrated every enclave of the social. In both producing and confessing to its illusionism, the Disney world epitomises a new relationship to experience that goes beyond leisure and entertainment. As Baudrillard has suggested, power now doubles back on itself to risk the real, to risk crisis in an attempt to manufacture real (political) stakes in the face of indifference and simulation. The presidency, during the Reagan era at least, was paradoxically the product of exactly the sort of media-enhanced Watergate simulacra that Reagan handled so 'ineptly' and yet have been so singularly unscandalous – one only has to think of 'Irangate', 'Contragate', 'Cocaine-gate', 'CIA-gate', 'Tailgate' etc. At the end of his presidency, Reagan's strength appeared to reside in his ability to impersonate an apparently real political figure who could only appear bland, when compared with the virtuosity of the imitation.

The presidency, like the real live animals that were originally intended to be a part of the Disneyland jungle ride, could never compete with the infallibility and fascination of the simulacrum. When Walt argued that 'we need mechanical animals, so that every boatload of people will see the same thing',[30] he was acknowledging the nature (in the double sense) of an era which regards 'nature' as secondary to the grounding experience of reproduction. Motivated by a nostalgia for a representational order that is now dead, the mechanical animals and figures are reanimated by investing them with a facsimile of life which suggests that the living are elsewhere. Appealing to a similar sort of fascination, both Disney and Reagan tell us that the technology of enactment can give us more reality than nature ever could. Umberto Eco has this in mind when he writes that, 'The pleasure of imitation, as the ancients knew, is one of the most innate in the human spirit: but here we not only enjoy a perfect imitation, we also enjoy the conviction that imitation has reached its apex and afterwards reality will always be inferior to it.'[31] The 'here' that he refers to, however, greatly exceeds the limited confines of the hyperreality that we observe as a feature of Disneylands. It is the here and now of the whole of the 'real' America, based as it is on a new ecology of fantasy and leisure, that marks the ascent of the simulacrum, the reign of the imitation, the twilight of the real.

In *Simulations*, Baudrillard provides the fullest account of the entanglement of the real with its representational model, and the 'perversity' of the relationship between the image and the referent. Opening with the Borgesian allegory of simulation, in which the cartographic account of the Empire becomes coextensive with the 'real' that it set out to describe, Baudrillard's analysis is of a postmodern culture of simulation. Disneyland is, of course, the paradigmatic model of this new order of equivalence. The caves at Lascaux, which, under the pretext of saving the original, were reconstructed as an exact replication just 500 metres from the site of the original, provide another example of a submission to simulation that is shared with Disneyland. Closer to home we might think of the proposal made in the 1970s to build an exact replica of Stonehenge in polystyrene – 'Foamhenge' – the perfect and hyperreal backdrop for our celluloid memories. What is significant about this sort of duplication is not that the memory of the original is progressively lost – an argument which as Baudrillard points out is utterly specious – but rather that the very fact of duplication is sufficient to render both artificial. So it is with Disneyland. The Disney scenario does not function to distance us from the 'real' unmediated facts of American life. Nor does it corrode faith and memory in the 'real' uncolonised imagination of the child. Rather it relegates the reality principle to a single plane of signification that recognises only equivalence and answers solely to the hyperreal aesthetics of duplication.

As the 'paradigmatic model of the entangled orders of simulation', Disneyland can no longer be regarded in the ideological terms delineated by either Dorfman and Mattelart, or the critical biographer Richard Schickel, as simply a panegyric to American values. To do so is to disguise its actuality as a third order simulacrum by attempting to restore the objective processes. Of the three 'orders of simulation' identified by Baudrillard, the first two – in which the sign is seen either to reflect or to mask and pervert an underlying and basic reality – belong to a theology of truth and secrecy that remains faithful to the reality principle sought by traditional ideological analysis. The third order, which 'masks the absence of a basic reality and in its ultimate form bears no relation to any reality whatsoever: it is its own pure simulacrum',[32] is the order of Disney America.

As a simulacrum, Disney America can no longer be treated as a perversion of a basic America that has any more legitimate claims to the principles either of truth or of reality. In its refusal to recognise or acknowledge any equivalence between the real and its sign, simulation is not simply another form of representation that has been cast adrift from the mooring of the referent: it is in fact radically opposed to all representation. The difference, in Baudrillard's words, is that: 'Whereas representation tries to absorb simulation by interpreting it as false representation, simulation envelops the whole edifice of representation as simulation.'[33] In this sense the Disney empire, if it can be said to conceal anything, is there to conceal the fact that it is the 'real' country, all of 'real' America that is Disneyland. (As Baudrillard points out, the Foucauldian analysis of prisons rests on a similar inversion; they serve to conceal the fact that it is the social in its entirety – apart from its institutions of deterrence and confinement (prisons, asylums, etc.) – that is in fact carceral.) So, when the visitor leaves his or her car and enters the Disney world, faith is restored in the 'reality' as opposed to the simulated hyperreality of the surrounding country – the habitus of the banality of the everyday. In this sense the parks take on the aspect of a subterfuge. For, as we have seen, 'it is no longer a question of a false representation of reality (ideology), but of concealing the fact that the real is no longer real, and thus of saving the reality principle ... The Disneyland imaginary is neither true nor false: it is a deterrence machine set up in order to rejuvenate in reverse the fiction of the real.'[34]

Here in Disney culture, the fascination lies in the intuition that, as simulacra, the images precede reality to the extent that they invert the causal and logical order of the real and its reproduction. Reality itself becomes contaminated by the artifice of the image in the double sense of having become both 'unnatural' (the image progressively eroding its *a priori* claims) and aestheticised. However, the metaphor of contamination fails to acknowledge the nature of the happy cancer that the Disney scenario celebrates. To see the infantile degeneration of the imaginary as the opiate of the leisure-consuming masses is, once again, to invoke an area of uncontaminated reality constellated around the terms of serious activities of work, politics, education and religion. But, as we have seen, it is precisely the infantile nature of the Disney experience that allows us to believe, as adults, that we inhabit a real world, in which play is replaced by seriousness, and consumed experience by self-determination.

What traditional critiques miss, in claiming that the 'Disney' parent nostalgically appropriates the natural disposition of the child in order to conceal the guilt arising from his or her own fall from grace, is the loss of the dialectic between the image(inary) and reality that previously upheld their distinction. For although the child does become a surrogate through which the adult receives absolution, engagement with the Disney imaginary, far from being escapist, can be seen as an attempt to restore the oppositional balance that allows more serious activities to be viewed as if they were contained within the confines of an external reality. In this sense, the escapist element of the Disney experience, if indeed there is one, is the desire to escape the nature and effects of a totally pervasive hyperreality. The paradox that emerges is that the images that we consume describe an equal impossibility of either a real or an imaginary – in other words their representational status can never be 'fixed'.

In Disney world we find a philosophy which eats out of one's hand. The mainstays of 'discerning' nineteenth-century epistemology, the 'real' itself and its significant other 'truth', have been killed off by the cancerous proliferation of late capitalist symbolic production. Lifestyle, and now history, are no longer merely canonised through images, but are constituted within and across them. Easy pickings perhaps, for peripatetic European semioticians searching for the totally inauthentic, the 'ultimate fake' to seal their apocalyptic deconstructions of postmodern culture at the nexus of history and representation. Here we might join Ed Cohen in the view that even Eco and Baudrillard, the great disclaimers of difference, as tourists of the baroque logic of Disney world and Disney America, have taken with them on their travels (in hyperreality) the clandestine 'other' of European value. In other words the fascination with the relationship between reality and falsity is in part motivated by a vestigial desire to assert the 'reality' of European culture – and this of course includes the truth/reality of proclamations made by Euro-intellectuals with regard to less authentic cultures than their own – as against the omnipresent falsity of American culture.

The spectre of the Frankfurt emigrees is raised once again. It is a spectre that perhaps points to two unbridgeable ways of thinking or to epistemologies born of very distinct cultures – a point that Baudrillard at least hints at:

> If it is negativity, irony and the sublime that govern European thinking, it is paradox which dominates that of America, the paradoxical humour of an achieved materiality, of an ever renewed self-evidence, of a bright new faith in the legality of the *fait accompli* which we always find amazing, the humour of a naive visibility of things, whilst we operate in the uncanny realm of the *deja vu* and the glaucous transcendence of history.[35]

But the lesson that Disney world as an allegory of postmodernism offers us must surely be seen in terms of the seduction of those total systems that answer only to the new consumer ecology of fantasy and desire. However, what is so often missed is that it is an 'ecology' that has gained considerable currency (in the double sense) within Europe, and specifically within the UK. In killing notions of truth, reality and history, simulation also re-surrects their 'corpses' as signs of the meaning that they can no longer possess. This is happening in England no less than in America, where historical simulation has effected a sort of 'Invasion of the Heritage Sna-tchers' more than adequately described by Richard Hewison.[36] Theme parks, far from being the substitute for American false/non-history, may well transpire to be the epitaph of European real/actual history. Within this frightening (ob)scenario, transcendence of any sort – glaucous or other-wise – must be viewed with a certain amount of suspicion, for there are as many indications in Europe as in America that simulation and the 'dis-neyfication' of culture have killed our illusion of otherness. In the theme parks of Europe, and the theme park that *is* Europe, as much as in stamping grounds of the intellectuals that Europe exports, the progressive erasure of all difference and contradiction that comes with the thematis-ation of cultural life has led to a curiously bleak sort of utopia. Any residual cultural disdain must immediately be swallowed. For it is on *both* (first world) sides of the Atlantic that (postmodern) death has found its ideal home.

The coordinates of criticism, of history and temporality, of the real and the imaginary, appear lost in the non-space of postmodernity that the Disney theme parks epitomise. However, this is not a non-space in the sense of being a void, but rather a utopian celebration of disappearance as the liberation of the pleasure principle of consumption. Writing about the nature of this type of experience can no longer be positioned outside it. All that the reader is left with is description, which itself conforms to the same principles of deadness and hypervisibility. In this case, maybe the Disney culture that is being described will only respond to an equally 'disneyfied' type of theory. For, as I hope has been made clear throughout this chapter, Disney is the model of a postmodern culture in which you have to be buried alive in order to survive. After all how can one describe disappearance without nostalgically invoking and resurrecting the absent object? As Barthes realised: ' "Capturing life" really means "seeing dead". Adjectives are the tools of this delusion: whatever else they may be saying, their very descriptive quality makes them funereal.'[37] In this sense the fascination of Disney is the fascination of being seduced by a dead object. This is the 'magic of disappearance', the 'paralysed frenzy' of the image that Baudrillard so cunningly invokes. What we are left with is a pornographic culture of obscenity and hypervisibility for which we are no longer permitted the absolution of disdain. This is the Disneyland of global first-world culture. And, although this text cannot be positioned outside that world, we can in conclusion agree with Baudrillard regarding the nature of the experience:

> One can, however, say that solicitation and greed have created out of it [the desire for fascination] disproportionately inflated images. These have become our real sex objects, the objects of our desire, and it is this substitution, this confusion (between desire and its materialised equivalent in images, not only sexual desire, but cognitive desire and its materialised equivalent in 'information', the desire to dream and its materialised equivalent in all the Disneylands of the world, the desire for space and its materialised equivalent in the programmed movement of 'two-weeks paid vacation', the desire for recreation and its programmed equivalent in home video equipment, etc.) that gives rise to the obscenity of our culture.[38]

Notes

1 Dick Hebdige, 'The Bottom Line on Planet One: Squaring Up to the Face'. First published in *Ten 8* no.19. Republished in *Hiding in the Light* (Comedia, 1988) (Footnotes refer to this second publication).
2 Hebdige, 'The Bottom Line on Planet One', p.158.
3 Ibid., p.159.
4 Samuel R. Delany, *Babel 17* (Gollancz, 1967).
5 Jean Baudrillard, *Simulations* (Semiotext(e), 1983), p.145.
6 Ed Cohen, 'The "Hypereal" v the "Really Real": If European Intellectuals Stop Making Sense of American Culture can we still Dance?', *Cultural Studies*, 1989, p.25.
7 Dorfman and Mattelart, *How to Read Donald Duck – Imperialist Ideology in the Disney Comic* (I.G. Editions, 1975).
8 Frederic Jameson, 'The Cultural Logic of Late Capitalism', *New Left Review*, no. 146, Jul/Aug 1984.
9 Dorfman and Mattelart, *How to Read Donald Duck*, p.33.

10 Ibid., p.34.
11 See Baudrillard, 'The Clone Story of an Artificial Child' in *ZG*, no. 11, Summer 1984.
12 Jorges Luis Borges, *The Book of the Sand and The Gold of Tigers – Selected Late Poems* (Penguin, 1979).
13 Dorfman and Mattelart, *How to Read Donald Duck*, p.34.
14 Jameson, 'The Cultural Logic of Late Capitalism', p.72.
15 See Louis Althusser: *Essays on Ideology* (Verso, 1984).
16 Baudrillard, *Simulations*, p.48.
17 Richard Schickel, *The Disney Version: the Life, Times, Art and Commerce of Walt Disney* (1968).
18 See Paul Taylor, 'The Disney State', *Art and Text*, 27 and *File*, 25, joint issue 1986.
19 In Bob Thomas, *Walt Disney: An American Original* (Gulf and Western, 1976) p.257.
20 Guy Debord, 'Society of the Spectacle', *Red and Black* (Rebel Press, 1983) Section 4.
21 Schickel, *The Disney Version*, p.325.
22 Taylor, 'The Disney State', p.55.
23 Umberto Eco, *Travels in Hyperreality* (Picador, 1986) p.43.
24 Debord, 'Society of the Spectacle'.
25 Eco, *Travels in Hyperreality*, p.26.
26 Walt Disney's own term for the existing 'leisure-parks' that Disneyland was intended to displace.
27 Taylor, 'The Disney State'.
28 Quoted in Schickel, *The Disney Version*, p.325.
29 Archibald Macleish. Quotation memorialised on a plaque in the 'Hall of America' EPCOT centre, Florida.
30 Thomas, *Walt Disney: An American Original*, p.263.
31 Eco, *Travels in Hyperreality*, p.44.
32 Baudrillard, *Simulations*, p.11.
33 Ibid., p.25.
34 Ibid.
35 Jean Baudrillard, *America* (Verso, 1988) p.84.
36 See Richard Hewison, *The Heritage Industry*.
37 Roland Barthes quoted in Maeghan Morris, 'Room 101 or a Few Worst Things in the World' in *Seduced and Abandoned*, ed. Frankovits (Stonemoss, 1984) p.95.
38 Jean Baudrillard, 'What are You Doing After the Orgy?', *Artforum*, Oct 1983.

8 Space on Flat Earth: *Blade Runner*

Dystopia revisited

In an article entitled, 'A Report from the Western Front', Dick Hebdige elaborates his view of second world postmodernity, introducing the discussion via the life and work of the science fiction writer Philip K. Dick:

> When Dick was alive, he lived in Santa Ana, California just a few miles from Disneyland. In fact he lived so close that when he was alive, he would sometimes describe himself in interviews and lectures as the spokesperson for Disneyland. One day he went there to meet his friend and fellow SF writer, Norman Spinrad. The two men talked about Watergate on the deck of Captain Hook's pirate ship. The same day Dick discussed the rise of fascism with Spinrad as they were spun around inside a giant teacup. (Elizabeth Entebi headed the crew that filmed these exchanges for Paris TV.) Dick used to think a lot about simulation then. He could never forget the fact that he knew how to get from his apartment to Disneyland and that Disneyland was in some strange way the home of the obsessions that drove him to write. He used to worry a lot in those days about how to draw the line between reality and fiction, copies and originals, the authentic and the inauthentic.[1]

It is these very same preoccupations that permeate my own discussion of Disney world and that find their almost literal visualisation in the film *Blade Runner* (based on a novel by Dick), which forms the second part of this allegorical excursion into the 'second world' of postmodernity.

It is a world in which the gravitational pull of the 'real' has been thrown into crisis, as simulation increasingly corrodes any chance of spontaneous or unreflexive faith in any ability to 'situate' ourselves within a new landscape of instability and flux. The boundary terms have changed, as has the old (humanist) cartography with its projections, grids and perspectives. Deprived of stable coordinates or reliable reference points the 'second world', represented initially by Disney and now by the film *Blade Runner*, would appear to offer no possibility of inflection across its surfaces, no textures to impede a vertiginous slide that knows neither beginning nor end. But despite the Moebian topology of postmodernism, which designates a contiguity of the close and the distant, exterior and interior, the object and the subject in the same infinite spiral, we find in Disney and *Blade Runner* a separation of possibility, a forking of the paths across this treacherous image-thin surface. For as allegories of our postmodern future-present we are offered alternately celebration and caution.

Attempting to expand the nature of his concerns and preoccupations as a science fiction writer, Dick found himself up against a number of questions: What is the domain of the science fiction writer? What does the science fiction writer know about, and on what topic is s/he an authority? In response he was to say that 'I can't claim to be an authority on anything, but I can honestly say that certain matters absolutely fascinate me, and I write about them all the time. The two basic topics that fascinate me are "What is reality?" and "What constitutes the authentic human being?" '[2] No two matters could be more prescient to an account of postmodernism, nor could the ramifications be better mirrored (or screened) upon the surfaces of Disney world and *Blade Runner*.

Both allegories represent experience as it unfolds within the already familiar second world topography that we find delineated within the four constitutive terms of simulation, authenticity, history and subjectivity. However, the relations established within these terms are radically different. The obscenity of the Disney experience resides not in its lack of authenticity as a cultural product (a verdict that would have validity only if the experience belonged to an era of reproduction not simulation) but rather in the utopian nature of its attempt to 'domesticate' the sign. Like any culture of simulation, the proximity and transparency of the sign leads one to suspect that what is being deified – in the case of Disney' a sanitised account of American history – is being deified only because it has achieved stability through its own death. What is frightening about this vision is that it is utopian only in that it celebrates liberation from the vicissitudes of life.

In contrast, the second world depicted in *Blade Runner*, corresponds to a very different vision of our postmodern future. The endlessly proliferating sign that in Disney serves to reassure the consumer of the authenticity of his/her position within the apparently comprehensible system of consumer signification (with all its *connotations* of choice, superabundance, etc.), has, in *Blade Runner*, been replaced by scarcity and uncertainty. The domesticated sign, instead of becoming the armchair of the leisure class, is constantly interrogated, scrutinised and deconstructed as its claims to transparency and authenticity are called into question. History is fought over the few signifiers of the past that continue to circulate and maintain claims to the referent. In this world, signs no longer function simply as the interchangeable units in a Moebian twist that unifies the past and the future in a seamless present, but are scrutinised and contested as the very foundation of our existence and self-knowledge. In *Blade Runner*, to own these signs is to own the right to life.

The film is ostensibly set in Los Angeles in the year 2019. However, it is an indeterminate city set in an equally indeterminate future. According to Syd Mead, the design consultant for *Blade Runner*: 'One of the principles behind designing this film is that it should be both forty years in the future and forty years in the past.'[3] The result is what he terms 'retro-deco'. This is the aesthetic espoused by Robert Venturi and Denise Scott-Brown in *Learning from Las Vegas* predicated on the glorification of the billboard strip, the ruthless schlock of casino culture and the denial of all historical or temporal specificity in favour of the immediacy and neon novelty of the recontextualised sign. It is an urban trend that finds its contemporary apotheosis in the newly proposed 'Trump Castle' (designed by Philip Johnson and John Burgee) – a medievalised skyscraper comprising of six coned and crenellated cylinders, plated in gold leaf and surrounded by a real moat and drawbridges – designed for Gotham City's own JR, billionaire developer Donald Trump. Trump's castle, like the neo-Egyptian headquarters of the Tyrell Corporation (the seat of power in the LA of *Blade Runner*) represent a logic of social control based on the hegemony of unfettered financial power.

In contrast the surrounding environment, inhabited by the 'little people', the casbah of the indigenous city is represented by a different sort of 'retro-deco'. Stripped of the signification of power, it appears as a post-industrial aesthetic combining accretion and decay. Rejecting the ultra-modernity represented by the space ship/station Mead and Scott sought in this surrounding architectural landscape to expose the technological heart of darkness that shadows those narratives of progress that still legitimate our expansionist and colonial ambitions. The ground-level streets escape the logic of power that emanates from the corporate panopticans way above them. The street is organic, combining and cross-referencing first and third world peoples and technologies – but it is also explosive as the two critical masses meet at the point of fusion. Like the 'American street' described by Baudrillard, it lacks the 'historical stability' of the European street which finds its past inscribed in its architecture, the ebbs and flows of its people, the nature of its transactions. Instead it is a street which is witness to a peculiar sort of violence, a violence of hyper-visibility: '. . . it [the American street] is always turbulent, lively kinetic, and cinematic, like the country itself, where the specifically historical and political stage counts for little but where change, whether spurred by technology, racial differences, or the media, assumes virulent forms: its violence is the violence of a very way of life.'[4] The omnipresent and corrosive rain, the neo-baroque lighting, and the flawed voice-over narration conjure a Chandleresque image of streets which below the neo-baroque edifice of the Tyrell Corporation are 'dark with something more than night.' The metropolis itself is therefore both postindustrial and postmodern. Everything in the city space speaks of a recycling process that denies linguistic, architectural or geographical specificities. Its architects, like its inhabitants, are style cannibals seeking assertion, totemism, and segregation via the medium of the 'neo'. Perhaps inspired in part by Fritz Lang's celebrated vision in *Metropolis*, made in 1926, the city operates on many levels; the upper echelons of society and transportation systems, as in the Lang film, are 'at least sixty stories above street level' and only the 'little people' circulate amongst the omnipresent detritus down below. Lang is also influential in that he introduces Orientalism into our vision of the future. The blinking neon signs, the oriental music and atmosphere of the bars, the exchange beween the blankness of a Coke advert and the seductive inscrutability of an Oriental face, all speak to us of the end of the arrogant autonomy of the West. The linearity of Western script itself collapses into the much more iconic form of the semiogram. Here we find ourselves within the 'Empire of Signs' that is so vividly described by Roland Barthes.

In a book written by Dominique Laporte, *Histoire de la Merde*,[5] he makes the claim that the production of waste has, since industrialism, been the index of the healthy functioning of those productive and reproductive systems that form an economy. In the postindustrial scenario of *Blade Runner*, waste takes on a new significance. Decay no longer takes place according to the ordered and anticipated programmes of obsolescence. It now creates its own logic as the internal time of those processes that were proper to industrialism are accelerated beyond production and into simulation. Nothing escapes this logic. The buildings themselves have developed according to a process of continual accretion whereby the additional parts themselves become the functioning organs of their otherwise wasted anatomies. This is the logic of architectural prosthesis. The destiny of modern architecture, which according to Mies van der Rohe was to 'translate the will of an epoch into space' has been abandoned. Where the classical modernist skyscraper romanticised corporate bureaucracy and mass production, the buildings of *Blade Runner* have lost any organic or expressive relationship to emerging technology. Instead they look to industrial effluence and detritus for their inspiration and materials. We find architectural idealism replaced by material pragmatism. In the crowded cityspace it is, after all, both easier and cheaper to recycle obsolete architectural 'waste' than to demolish it.

Even one of the characters, the figure of J. F. Sebastian, who though only 25 years old is wrinkled and utterly delapidated, is submitted to this process of advanced decay. He, like the city, suffers from what the replicant Pris describes as 'accelerated decrepitude'. It is a sort of atrophy and inertia that occurs at the moment at which change has reached its terminal velocity, and can from that point on only double back and consume itself. J. F. Sebastian and the city have reached this point. Suffering from the pathology of the 'post', they are both new and in ruins.

It is this process of recycling that makes the cityscape truly postmodern. Everywhere, the sign is recontextualised. The signifier is separated from the signified in a way that exactly recalls the poststructuralist account of the text. The inhabitants of this future LA are also the inhabitants of the second world described by Hebdige: 'a motley gang of bricoleurs, ironists, designers, publicists, image consultants, hommes et femmes fatales, market researchers, pirates, adventurers, flaneurs and dandies'.[6] Punks, Krishnas and Oriental merchants appear as gross self-parodies as their consumption and manipulation of the codes becomes a desperate attempt to keep abreast of the empire of signs that surrounds them, and to regain a hold on any signifying practice that can in some way reclaim identity. In this infinitely mutable and indeterminate environment, where even the language (cityspeak) becomes 'a mishmash of Japanese, Spanish, German, what have you', the self is utterly and self-consciously dispersed in representation. Recovery, as we shall see, can only take place through those same practices.

The representational space of the city speaks of a recycling that quotes not only from different spatial structures – there are recognisable elements of LA, New York, Tokyo, Hong Kong, etc. – but also from different temporal structures. It therefore represents a new relationship to space and time that is also uniquely postmodern. Roman and Greek columns mix with recurring signs from classical Oriental mythology in a hybrid of old and new. Here pastiche becomes the dominant aesthetic – an aesthetic of quotation which, unlike parodic quotation, is without attribution or reference. In Jameson's words:

> Pastiche is, like parody, the imitation of a peculiar or unique style, the wearing of a stylistic mask, speech in a dead language: but it is a neutral practice of such mimicry, without parody's ulterior motive, without the satirical impulse, without laughter, without that still latent feeling that there exists something normal compared to which what is being imitated is rather comic.[7]

In *Blade Runner* the stage sets intermingle freely with an architectural history that itself has become staged – a supermarket of stylistic convention. Elements from 'real' architectural history (the Ennis-Brown house designed by Frank Lloyd Wright), those from cinematic history (the 1929 set called 'New York Street', used in a number of Humphrey Bogart and James Cagney movies) and simulated architectural styles coalesce to produce a synthetic meta-pastiche. The result is an excess of scenography – an obscene transparency – a pornographic violence in which everything is rendered as performance.

It is within this (ob)scenario that the narrative of the film is enacted. Based loosely on a science fiction novel by Philip K. Dick called, *Do Androids Dream of Alien Sheep?* the film is set in an utterly Baudrillardian world. It is a world in which 'The real is produced from miniaturised units, from matrices, memory banks and command models – and with these it can be reproduced an indefinite number of times.'[8] In command of the reproductive processes that generate the real is the Tyrell Corporation, primarily responsible for the creation of 'replicants' – genetically engineered human simulacra, 'skin jobs' designed for use 'off-world as slave labour in the hazardous exploration and colonisation of other planets'. With the latest generation of replicants, the 'Nexus 6', the reproduction of the real has exceeded its production to create beings that 'are superior in strength and agility and at least equal in intelligence to the genetic engineers who created them'. They are 'more human than human' in every way except one, and for this they are prepared to risk 'retirement' – hyper-reality's euphemistic term for execution. They lack only history.

This lack is interrogated through the medium of the image, and a ('Voight Com') test designed to measure the degree of emotional reaction that is elicited in response to questions regarding the suspect's personal history. The investigative process is always via the TV/video screen. Screening takes on a double meaning – it is both the surface upon which the narrative action takes place, and the process of discrimination between the authentic and the inauthentic, human and replicant. Established in one of the very early shots in which the background cityscape is superimposed across the full-size image of an iris, the screen displaces the retina as the origination of the image – TV becoming the nether-eye (never I). Nothing escapes codification on the screen, which is the centre of control and of knowledge. The test probes, decomposes and restructures the signifiers of the past and of the subject, on a screen that collapses the polling process into the referendum. It reveals 'a truth which is no longer the reflexive truth of the mirror, nor the perspective truth of the panoptic system and of the gaze, but the manipulative truth of the test which probes and interrogates, of the laser that touches and then pierces, of computer cards which retain your punched out sequences, of the genetic code which regulates your combination of cells which inform your sensory universe.'[9] Baudrillard's description of contemporary testing procedure corresponds exactly to the sort of tests conducted by Deckard. Ironically, such testing circumvents its own purpose, since history and subjectivity can never exceed the codification that the test is designed to dismantle.

In *Camera Lucida*, Roland Barthes makes the claim that 'History is hysterical: it is constituted only if we consider it, only if we look at it – and in order to look at it we must be excluded from it . . . That is the time when my mother was alive before me is – History.'[10] As Giuliana Bruno points out in an excellent article on *Blade Runner*[11] what constitutes history for Barthes is also history for the replicants. They return to earth to recover what they have been excluded from, in a double sense. In having no past, no history, they are excluded from the very possibility of exclusion. In other words they are condemned to living in a perpetual present. Their predicament therefore belongs to all of us who are unwilling to impose depth upon the simulacrum. In the world of signs that they inhabit, an age of soft technologies of genetic and mental 'software' the mere possession of human emotions (which in traditional science fiction are the signifying boundary between the authentic human and the android) is no longer any guarantee of authenticity. What they return to seek is the symbolic area of exclusion, of genesis and Oedipal development, that restores the temporal dimension to experience, and that for Barthes is both our history and our identity.

In searching for their past the replicants are inevitably caught in the double bind of representation and reproduction. As simulacra, they are themselves 'copies for which there are no originals' and yet, in order to discover their own identity, they face the seemingly impossible task of making the reproductions and copies that are our history yield an original, or 'real', that is absent from their lived experience. Only Rachel escapes this double bind. For she is in the unique position of not knowing whether she is a replicant or not. It is her doubt that casts aspersions on the authenticity of the Blade Runner Deckard's own claims to history and identity, and ultimately generates their love affair which itself is born out of an empathetic understanding of each other's doubts. When Deckard asserts his own human identity by killing the replicant 'other' Zhora, and then returns to his apartment with the disturbed Rachel, he observes that, 'replicants weren't supposed to have feelings, but then again nor were Blade Runners'. Indeed, during Rachel's very first encounter with Deckard she asks him whether or not he has himself taken the test that supposedly distinguishes the real from the fake. As the stability of these distinctions between 'real' and 'fake', the 'self' and the 'other' falters, so faith in the validity of his own self is eroded. Fear of the replicants is therefore a fear of the double and the signification of death that accompanies it. As Baudrillard points out, 'To begin to resemble the other, to take on their appearance, is to seduce them, since it is to make them enter the realm of metamorphosis despite themselves.'[12] This seduction is, for Deckard, literal as well as metaphorical.

Within this Hades of simulation everything is subject to reversibility and absorption within its operational double, in the manner so vividly described by Baudrillard. When it is claimed that, 'Commerce is our goal here at Tyrell. More human than human is our motto,' Dr Tyrell and Professor Baudrillard meet under the same conditions of immanent reversibility. This reversibility reaches its apotheosis in Rachel who has internalised the signs and symptoms of her being to the point at which they become her actuality, the real terms of her existence. It is this psychosomosis that distinguishes her from Leon, who self-consciously attempts to feign a past that he never had in order to survive. Baudrillard, quoting Littre, explains this difference between simulation and dissimulation, using illness as a metaphor:

Someone who feigns an illness can simply go to bed and make believe
that he is ill. Someone who simulates an illness produces in himself some
of the symptoms.' Thus, feigning or dissimulating leaves the reality
principle intact: the difference is always clear, it is only masked: whereas
simulation threatens the difference between 'true' and 'false', between
'real' and 'imaginary'.[13]

The replicant Leon cannot answer questions about his mother/history
because the dissimulation of his past leaves the reality principle, against
which his claims to legitimacy and authenticity are judged, intact. Rachel
on the other hand survives because the symptoms that she produces are
internalised. Her claims to 'truth' are therefore indistinguishable from
those of 'real' human beings; to say that she simulates her symptoms, her
sexuality and memory is to say that she *realises* and experiences them. This
is the 'real' threat. For, 'simulation is infinitely more dangerous ... [than
"dissimulation" or "feigning"] since it always suggests, over and above its
object, that *law and order themselves might really be nothing more than a
simulation.*'[14]

However, it is not just psychosomosis that distinguishes Rachel from the
other replicants. She also has a document that attests to an identity that
endures over time. This document is in fact a photograph of her with her
mother. As in Barthes' reflections in *Camera Lucida*, the photograph of the
mother assumes importance as a link between the past, present and future.
In an age in which memory is only recognised through signification – once
it gains photographic similitude and enters what the French writer André
Malreaux termed the 'museum without walls' – the photograph becomes a
document of existence. It becomes history in the Foucauldian sense: it
transforms memories into monuments. It is simply, 'one way in which a
society recognises and develops the mass of documentation with which it is
inextricably linked'.[15] Photographs, for the replicants as well as their
adversary Deckard, constitute such documentation. Deckard understands
this when he finds the replicant Leon's photographs: 'I don't know why
replicants would collect photos. Maybe they were like Rachel, they needed
memories.' The photograph is both memory and eucharist. It redeems the
believer from his or her imprisonment within the perpetual present, providing the illusion of temporal continuity that is history – and for the
replicants their destiny.

The medium of photography thus gains significance as the Blade
Runner Deckard's only means of interrogating the suspected replicant's
claims to authenticity. The ubiquity of photographic or reproduced
imagery corresponds to the twofold function assigned to photography in
general by Susan Sontag when she claims that:

Cameras define reality in the two ways essential to the workings of an
advanced industrial society: as a spectacle (for masses) and as an object

of surveillance (for the rulers) ... Social change is replaced by a change in images. The freedom to consume a plurality of images and goods is equated with freedom itself ... As we make images and consume them, we need still more images; and still more.'[16]

Identity, history and reality coalesce on the surface of the print. Deckard's own catalogue of the past, displayed on a piano, is used to elicit anecdotal memories from Rachel, bonding them in a union of common childhood experience and nostalgia. Photography for the replicants constitutes the documentation of history. It is conceived as a medium in which the signifier and the referent are collapsed into one another. They assert the referent and its reality in the way described by Barthes: 'In photography I can never deny that "the thing has been there." There is a superimposition here of reality and of the past.'[17] For the replicants, as acknowledged by Tyrell, this functions to stabilise them in an otherwise volatile present: 'We began to recognise a strange obsession ... if we gift them with the past, we can create a cushion or pillow for their emotions, and consequently we can control them better.'

This cushion or pillow takes the form of a narrative space that allows us to locate the self within the terms of some sort of temporal continuity. This narrative space is, of course, our history. For the replicants history can only be recovered through representation – hence the fascination for the photograph. In this sense they provide an allegorical reading of our own postmodern condition. As Deckard reflects at the scene of the replicant Roy's death: 'All he wanted were the same answers the rest of us want. Where do I come from? Where am I going? How long have I got?' But for the replicants, these questions have a greater urgency. Incapable of being alienated, since they have no stable history to be alienated from, the total fragmentation and dispersal of replicant subjectivity in the signs that are their being means that their experience of the world is that of the schizophrenic. They are, to paraphrase Baudrillard, bereft of every scene and in this sense prey to an absolute proximity of experience that, as Lacan has shown us, results from an inability to experience the persistence of the 'I' over time. Unable to produce the limits of his or her own being, the replicant is 'now only a pure screen, a switching center for all the networks of influence.'[18]

The inability to locate the experience of the present within the larger set of experiences that constitute our biographical history has the effect of releasing it (present/time) from those activities and intentionalities that might make it the space of praxis. The present overwhelms and engulfs the subject, since he or she can achieve no distance from it. Because of this, the replicants suffer from the same peculiarly postmodern pathology of 'accelerated decrepitude' that was seen to be a feature of the genetic misfit

J. F. Sebastian and of the city itself. They suffer from what might be termed 'burn-out', in the most literal sense. All experience takes on an intoxicatory and hallucinogenic intensity, but as their creator Dr Tyrell 'poetically' points out; 'The light that burns twice as bright burns half as long, and you have burned so very brightly ...'

The light that burns is the light of the retinal image. The 'pure screen' that is the replicant/schizoid psyche offers no interpretative cushion that can absorb the imprint of the image as unmodulated sense data – the literal signifier in isolation. In this culture of the simulacrum, absolute primacy is accorded to the image, and therefore to vision and to the gaze. The replicant Roy realises this, and justifies himself to his creator Dr Tyrell, by appealing to his desire to synthesise what he has seen with the 'human' (non-schizoid) ability to order the image – 'If only you could have seen what I have seen with your eyes.' The eye is no longer the window to the soul – it is the soul. And for Roy, who blinds and kills his creator, Tyrell, it is the Bataillian nether-I (never-I) of the egg (the creative and originating source but also for Bataille a persistent metaphor for the eye) that is extinguished. By killing Tyrell in this way, Roy refuses symbolic castration – refuses acceptance of himself as the 'twinkle in his father's eye'.

To understand this Oedipal psychodrama, it is worth recapitulating the scenario out of which replicant/postmodern crisis of the self is born. The 'crisis' that is being enacted is the crisis of living in a world in which, as Baudrillard puts it:

> Something has changed, and the Faustian, Promethean (perhaps Oedipal) period of production and consumption has given way to the 'protienic' era of networks, to the narcissistic and protean era of connections contiguity feedback and generalised interface that goes with the universe of communication. With the television image – the television being the ultimate and perfect object for this era – our own body and the whole surrounding universe become a control screen.[19]

The problem that the replicants, like the postmodern subject, have to confront, is how to *produce* themselves and to give substantiality to their lives when history and in particular the means of self-historising, documenting or narrating the self have lost any 'real' credibility – when they too take on the depthlessness of simulation.

To understand the replicants' actions in the face of this predicament we must turn away from Freud – who underscores the historical significance of memory as the foundation of identity – and turn once again to Lacan. Lacan's account of schizophrenic experience as the breakdown of the signifying chain and a resultant inability to assimilate the present within the larger set of experiences that constitute the self, offers a route to understanding the way in which the replicants seek to escape the imprisonment of their condition. What has so far been omitted from this reading of Lacan is the psychoanalytical account of the subject's entry into the symbolic order via the familial and Oedipalising processes with which we are familiar from orthodox Freudian psychoanalysis. The search for the self that the replicants undertake is thus a search for origins within the pre-existent symbolic order. This takes on the character of an Oedipal journey. Only Rachel, who does not know if she is a replicant, succeeds. In assuming a sexual identity and acknowledging the paternal, the 'name of the father', she is guaranteed entry into the symbolic order that allows her to assume an identity in relation to the 'other'. For Leon, Pris, Zhora and ultimately Roy, the absence of the 'other' means that there is no mirror of the self against which various representations can be tested. In this way they apotheosise the most radical conception of the postmodern subject.

As we have seen, the Lacanian view is that coherent notions of selfhood emerge only with the subject's entry into the symbolic order, which itself is conceived as a function of language. 'The subject is born insofar as the signifier emerges in the field of the other. But by this very fact, this subject – which was nothing if not a subject coming into being – solidifies into a signifier.'[20] Neither of the male replicants, Leon or Roy, emerge from the field of the other. Leon's lack/identity is revealed only when interrogated about his Oedipal history – his mother. Roy, as we have seen, refuses symbolic castration and the acceptance of the law of the father – 'it is very difficult to meet your maker' – and in killing Dr Tyrell commits the ultimate Oedipal crime.

However, Roy's own fate suggests, or rather hints at, an alternative to the Lacanian view of subjectivity as a purely Oedipal/linguistic function. The oppositions between real/imaginary and self/other that were imploded into undifferentiated simulation in the early part of the film, as Deckard's own non-replicant identity falters in the face of an 'other' that, in the case of Rachel, literally merges with the self, are for narrative purposes revived in the central section, in which the replicants seek their Oedipal origins. Here the scene of absolute simulation and indifference is cast aside as the replicants seek the symbolic dimension that for Lacan is the prerequisite for an identity that can endure the passage of time. There is an irony to this quest since to accept what Lacan terms the Law – the name-of-the-father – may well (*pace* Deleuze and Guattari) be merely to accept the Oedipal straitjacket of simulated difference.

It is an irony that is not lost in the film as Roy's Oedipal journey finally proves to be a mistaken quest to seek the truth beneath the simulacrum. The reductive notion of identity that this quest implies is ultimately discarded perhaps because such a voyage still belongs to a theology of opposition – between latent and manifest or, in Lacanian terms, the movement from organic symptom to the unconscious or linguistic order – both of which invoke obsolete distinctions between truth and appearance. After all, given that the (postmodern) 'world' that *Blade Runner* describes is situated within the spatial logic of the simulacrum, why should the principle of simulation stop at the portals of the unconscious? It is an ambiguity that is reasserted in the penultimate scenes when the replicant Roy saves Deckard's life, preferring life over death even in the emptiness of a scenario that renders either meaningless.

The strength of the film lies in part in its refusal to impose a resolution upon the crisis of simulation. It is however a tormenting refusal that corresponds to what Elias Canetti has termed 'A tormenting thought: as of a certain point, history was no longer *real*. Without noticing it, all mankind suddenly left reality: everything happening since then was supposedly not true; but we supposedly didn't notice. Our task would now be to find that point, and as long as we didn't have it, we would be forced to abide in our present destruction.'[21] The replicants' search for their vanishing point in history fails. Neither history, nor reality nor identity is found. Instead of the self being revealed mnemonically – subjectivity being both 'found' and 'resolved' in the rubric of repressed childhood experience – the replicants find that the search for the self is a journey, a mental labyrinth that reveals only the absence of any minotaur. Although it is a journey that takes random and erratic courses and ultimately ends at impasses, this does not in itself negate either the urgency or the validity of the search. That history, reality and identity are *not* revealed to be lurking somewhere beneath the dissembling membrane of the image or in the Oedipal sanctioning of cultural conformity in the end (there is no end), doesn't matter. And instead we are offered a pact. It takes place between Deckard, the Blade Runner and Rachel, who believes but does not know that she exists in simulation. It is a pact that finds its echo in Philip K. Dick's own definition of reality in the face of his concern with simulation and the horror of the inauthentic: 'Reality', he claimed, 'is that which, when you stop believing it, doesn't go away.'[22] It also refuses to be named since it steps outside linguistic determinations of belief. When Deckard leaves the city with Rachel as his partner, Gaff, his 'blade running' sidekick's departing remarks are; 'It's too bad she won't live, but then again who does.' Rachel may be simulated, implying as it does 'limited longevity', but for Deckard this no longer matters. Whether she is or isn't, it must remain unspoken since to test it is to turn it into simulation – for their 'reality' to slide into inauthenticity. It must in other words remain a secret, since that is all they have:

The secret: the seductive and initiatory quality of that which cannot be said because it is meaningless, and of that which is not said even though it gets around. Hence I know the other's secret but do not reveal it, and he knows I know it but does not let it be acknowledged: the intensity between the two is simply the secret of the secret. This complicity has nothing to do with some hidden information. Besides even if the partners wished to reveal the secret they could not, since there is nothing to say ... [23]

Looking for difference on the 'second world'

In characterising the two views of the second world within the paired terms utopian and dystopian, it might seem as though one of the fundamental and distinguishing features of the 'second world' of postmodernity has been ignored – namely its loss of, or (in)difference. It is a world, if we remember, in which the referent is in a state of perdition and the image anticipates a reality that in fact never had the chance to precede it. The most distinctive feature of this world is therefore its flatness. For what it has lost is faith in the dialectic between reality and imagery to the point at which the image has achieved autonomy by taking over and imposing its own immanent and ephemeral logic. It is a logic without depth, a logic that collapses the distinctions between interiority and exteriority as everything is forced to submit to hyperrealisation within the simulacrum. Exploring the boundaries of this space through the two 'case studies' has in one sense the absurdity of the 'mad project' of the Borgesian tale, in which the cartographers of the empire dream of a coextensivity between the map and the territory – a dream which along with the mirror of the other disappears when submitted to the principle of simulation. However, what the comparison may reveal is that even within this second world system of immanent reversibility and (in)difference, the operational spaces that are created, although still aligned along a horizontal axis, none the less describe our postmodern condition in ways that remain strangely different. In other words, what I want to suggest is that the non-spaces of postmodernism that have been described, *can* in fact be mapped in ways that do not nostalgically or reactively contravene their status as simulacra.

Neither the Disney theme parks nor *Blade Runner* can be said to represent postmodernism or indeed some more distant postmodern future. After all, what is being re-presented? Is it simply a past that we never had, or that only ever existed in representation, or a future that is still to come? Which ever way one looks at it, the collapse of the temporal dimension in the face of the simulacrum leaves us with no present, since the present is everywhere, and equally no re-present-ation. Like the 'real', representation appears to belong to a previous era, now leaving us only with what Baudrillard has described as a large and useless body, that is both deserted and condemned. Access to the hyperreality that is postmodernism can only therefore come via a double coding that escapes the rigidity of the one-to-one relationship between image and reality, signifier and signified, that underlines any uninflected system of representation. One such system of double coding is to be found in allegory, and it is only in terms of an allegorical relationship to a past utopia and future dystopia that any comparison between the two studies can be made.

The temptation at this point is to indulge in the creation of a synthetic allegory that combines a 'disneyfied' account of the past, with the type of testing procedures that generate subjectivity out of history that are depicted in Ridley Scott's film. To suspend disbelief for a moment, it requires no great feat of the imagination to substitute the imaginary figure of Dr Tyrell with that of Walt Disney. After all, neither Disney nor Tyrell acknowledges the written text as history, and in both cases it is the photographic image that testifies to the authenticity of the past and the prescience of the present. In Disney world history only exists to the extent that it conforms to the dictate of the park's creator, that it can partake in the 'museum of living facts'. As has already been pointed out, the concept is itself paradoxical. Adorno[24] makes the point most succinctly when through the German word *museal* (museumlike), he establishes an etymological connection between the museum and the mausoleum. Disney's 'museum of living facts', is in fact the sepulchre of history – exactly the version of the past (unsuccessfully) meted out by Tyrell as a 'cushion or pillow' for the replicants' emotions. In both cases, history is administered (to echo Tyrell) as a 'gift' and thus as a means of social control. Packaging the past in this way ensures its position within an economy of leisure rather than politics, thereby annexing a future that can amount to nothing more than a repetition of the dead forms of the past. In this way Disney replaces history with self-perpetuating necromancy.

But for the replicants depicted in *Blade Runner* the photograph acts not as substitute but as subterfuge for the history that they never had, and this provides a clue to the nature of difference on 'planet two'. For the Oedipal odyssey that ultimately leads them to the man/men who fabricate the bounds of their experience (Disney/Tyrell), is motivated by a sense of loss. Even though the desire that is generated out of such a sense of loss may itself be a simulacrum, based on a psychoanalytical schema that creates rather than explains it – that it exists at all would seem to suggest that there are alternative ways of consuming the type of experiences that form the terrain of 'planet two'. Where the sanitisation and domestication of the sign in Disney is celebrated, in *Blade Runner* it is deplored. The mistake in casting Disney as the 'real' Tyrell figure of our century, is that what inevitably emerges is some sort of conspiracy theory. However, as we have seen, as a purely second world phenomenon, Disney commodifies fun not alienation. Once again we are forced back onto the difficult problem of desire and the way that it relates to the question of why a 'disneyfied' account of history, divorced from its referent, should, in this allegorical reading, be capable of offering two apparently incompatible readings, thereby seeming to deny the principles of flatness and immanent reversibility that supposedly locate the two cases in the 'second world'.

What exactly are the two allegorical conceptions of the future-present and where do they lead? The answer, I believe, lies in the framing context in which the operations of simulation take place. In Disney world the imaginary is *realised* by means of signifiers that no longer pertain to the referent. Where the referent appears still to be in operation in the 'real' non-Disney world, it is resurrected in a mummified form, which resists all operations of the subject upon it. The process of realisation thus also entails domestication, and it is this that is the utopian component of the Disney operation. In Disney the consumer is *realised* as a living satellite in a position of perfect and remote sovereignty in quotidian space. It describes a future landscape suffocatingly regimented and totally eventless. In other words, utterly boring.[25]

Like Disney, the 'scene' of *Blade Runner* is entirely that of simulation, but it is a scene that accommodates tensions – tensions between the second world understanding that the simulacrum conceals nothing, and the desire to invest the empty form of the simulacra with at least the vestiges of first world meaning. The success of *Blade Runner* lies in its ability to invoke the 'first world' as a difference component of the second, without becoming in the process an equally empty, nostalgic referential. The metaphysics of *real* and *authentic* values, perhaps hidden behind alienation, fetishism and 'false consciousness', are in this context (unlike that of Disney) collapsed under the urgent labour of finding, establishing and recognising oneself within this world. It succeeds in this because it manages to interrogate the particular moment at which simulation merges with that which it simulates. In doing so, it allows the intrusion of irony. The frame of reference that is invoked is not reality but simulation itself: what we view in the cinema is already a totally simulated reality where humans conform to stereotypes as much as replicants, both being coded in an eclectic mixture of movie genres and period styles. It is this double coding that distinguishes the second world of *Blade Runner* from the second world of Disney.

Notes

1 Dick Hebdige, 'A Report from the Western Front', *Block*, 12, 1986/87, p.6.
2 Philip K. Dick, 'How to Build a Universe that Doesn't Fall Apart Two Days Later' in *I Hope I Shall Arrive Soon* (Grafton, 1988) p.8.
3 Christopher Frayling, 'Grand Illusions', lecture series, RCA.
4 Jean Baudrillard, *America* (Verso, 1988) p.18.
5 See Dominique Laporte's *Histoire de la Merde* (Christian Bourgeois) 1978, and also, though now somewhat dated, Vance Packard's *Waste Makers* (Pelican 1960).
6 Hebdige, 'The Bottom Line on Planet One: Squaring up to the Face' in *Hiding in the Light* (Comedia, 1988) p. 159.
7 Frederic Jameson, 'Postmodernism and Consumer Society' in Foster (ed.), *Postmodern Culture* (Pluto, 1985) p. 114.
8 Jean Baudrillard, 'Simulations' p.3 Semiotext(e) N.Y. 1983.

9 ibid p.52.
10 Roland Barthes, 'Camera Lucida' p.65 N.Y. Hill and Wang 1981.
11 Giuliana Bruno, 'Ramble City, Postmodernism and Blade Runner' October – Summer 1987.
12 Jean Baudrillard, 'The Evil Demon of Images' p.15 Power Institute Publications.
13 Baudrillard, 'Simulations' p.5.
14 ibid p. 5/6.
15 Michel Foucault, 'Archiology of Knowledge' p.7 Tavistock 1972.
16 Susan Sontag, 'On Photography' p. 178–179 Allen Lane, London 1978.
17 Barthes, 'Camera Lucida' p.76.
18 Baudrillard, 'Ecstacy of Communication' p. 133 Foster ed 'Postmodern Culture'.
19 ibid p. 127.
20 Jaques Lacan, 'Four Fundamental Concepts of Psychoanalysis' p. 199 Penguin 1979.
21 Elias Canetti, 'The Human Province' p.69 N.Y. Seabury 1978.
22 Philip K. Dick, 'How to build a Universe that desn't fall apart two days later' p.10.
23 Baudrillard, 'On Seduction' p. 159 in Poster ed. 'Jean Baudrillard, Selected Writings' Polity 1988.
24 See T. W. Adorno, 'Valery Proust Museum' in 'Prisims' trans. Samuel and Shierry Weber, London Neville Spearman 1967.
25 This is also a conception of the future articulated and elaborated by J. G. Ballard. See interview in the 'Face' No.96 April 1988.

9 Reaching Degree Zero

Whichever way the analysis proceeds, one should be aware that it proceeds towards the glaciation of meaning, it aids the precession of simulacra and indifferent forms.

Jean Baudrillard, 'On Nihilism'

Recalling Baudrillard

According to Jean Baudrillard, something has changed. It is a change which is perverse and paradoxical, signalling the end of the very possibility of change. In the place of a world ordered according to monolithic truths, linear grids and representational stability, we are faced with a set of unstable and volatile equations that correspond to a collapsed or imploded representational space. Previously solid referents have been replaced by disorientating flux, stable subject positions by schizophrenic wanderings, steadfast relationships by the pragmatism and contingency of coalitions, calculated risks by terror, known dangers by the invisible reign of the unknown. With the liquefaction of all referentials we find the once sovereign space of the individual dissolved, encroached and invaded. No more space, no more fear and trembling. The abyss that Marlow looked into in Conrad's *Heart of Darkness* has become the site of a semiotic and psychoanalytical infill. Existential agrophobia has now been transformed into a sort of joyous claustrophobia born of an absolute proximity of the self to its various representations. No more reckonings with the self at the edge of the void, since the void itself has already been colonised. Reality, once deprived of its uniqueness, can only repeat itself – the feature film serialised and forced into the quotidean space of the soap opera. We find ourselves living in a world of uniform density in which the space of interaction has been replaced with the narcissism of contact, contiguity and feedback:

> We are no longer part of the drama of alienation; we live in the ecstasy of communication. And this ecstasy is obscene. The obscene is what does away with every mirror, every look, every image. The obscene puts an end to every representation. But it is not only the sexual that becomes obscene in pornography; today it is the whole pornography of information and communication, that is to say of circuits and networks, a pornography of all functions and objects in their readability, their fluidity,

132

their availability, their regulation, their forced signification, in their performativity, in their branching, in their polyvalence, in their free expression...[1]

This is Baudrillard's analysis, and perhaps condemnation, of the post-modern condition. It is an analysis that does not make direct claims to argument and substantiation, nor does it invoke the teleological principles by which traditional 'critical' discourse seeks to challenge and repudiate reality. Rather it operates at the level of insinuation, as a presence, which disappears like the hologram at the moment one seeks its substantiation. Like the 'real', the loss of which he constantly and paradoxically describes, Baudrillard's discourse is itself subordinated to the principles of transparency and equivalence that compromise the meaningfulness of those theoretical oppositions between public and private, subject and object, that had hitherto sustained critical theory. But, if theory can no longer offer itself as the mirror of the subject, what remains? What can it do? What charge of affect can it contain and transmit? What does it mean to engage with a theory that offers no positions except within its own 'cold lubricity'? Are we not simply seduced by a non-theory that in its futility consoles us in our abjection?

As the insinuation of uncertainty, or perhaps in its stronger form, a challenge to a reality of implosion, Baudrillard's discourse has been instrumental in shaping the view of postmodernity that emerges from this particular text. It is a discourse of seduction and disappearance. In part it is its refusal to be named, to as it were accept the critical name-of-the-father that allows the work of Baudrillard to step outside the parameters of critical debate. Whether condemned for its glacial turpitude or celebrated as the 'second coming' of a Messiah whose world has finally been delivered from the asphyxiating clutch of the referent, the Baudrillardian text no longer conforms or partakes in the ontology of traditionally established (post)modern debate. The taboos associated with unrestrained, hyperbolic hypothesis, and the refusal to be named, are both broken. As the guru of so-called radical postmodernists, the adulation that Baudrillard attracts must in part be due to the paradoxical ability to be ontologically outside a system in which the very terms of 'outside' and 'ontology' have been negated in advance by the system itself. However, more obviously the seduction of his work, like that of Foucault's, lies in its power. It is his power as the evil demon of the image – the Mephistopheles of the real – that induces this almost cabalistic reverence. It is to the nature of this magical complicity between reality and image that we shall now turn.

The three orders of simulacra

It is in conjuring the perversity of the relationship between the image and the referent that Baudrillard has assumed his present position as avatar of the postmodern condition. It is a perversity which confounds any naive faith in the transparency of images and takes the form of a secret – a complicity between the image and the thing. Any spontaneous confidence in the realism of images is shattered in the face of their 'diabolical conformity':

> The secret of the image (we are still speaking of contemporary technical image) must not be sought in its differentiation from reality, and hence in its representative value (aesthetic, critical or dialectical) but on the contrary in its 'telescoping' into reality, its short-circuit with reality, and finally in the implosion of image and reality.[2]

It is an implosion that leads us over the 'event horizon' of the real and directly into the simulated non-space of hyperreality. The 'real' is now redefined in terms of the media in which it moves. No longer anchored to the stable structures that had served to moor events to experiences and images to things, the real now floats in the indeterminate space between the recording and the playback. Like video tape – the recurrent metaphor of postmodern discourse – hyperreality cannot be confronted and 'read' directly, but instead must be approached obliquely in a way that mimics the helical scan of the video record and playback heads. What this emphasis on reproduction (and the already reproduced) entails is a shift in the locus of power, which no longer resides in the political economy, an economy of production, but in the *operational* structure of the codes within which commodity consumption is already programmed as spectacle. This transition, and the resultant trajectory of the real to the hyperreal, is charted through what Baudrillard terms the three orders of simulacra.

Periodised in terms of the 'early modern', 'modern' and 'postmodern', the three orders of simulacra are to be understood not as a universal history, but rather as an account of the changing referent or alibi of social value, and the functioning logic of the societies that such value represents. (It is a genealogy based on a critique of Marx's account of the development of capital found in *The Poverty of Philosophy*.)

Early modernity, according to Baudrillard, supersedes feudal society, which he characterises in terms of a static social space in which things – the real, social status, etc. – function unequivocally. Here, the unquestioned positioning of each individual in a determinate social space allows the sign to operate with a total transparency and clarity. The order of things is guaranteed and 'any confusion of signs is punished'.[3] However, with the breakdown of the caste order, what emerges is a bourgeoisie prepared to engage in 'open competition of the level of the distinctive signs'.[4] This marks the end of the era of the 'obliged sign' and the birth of representation and the 'early modern' period.

'Early modernity' is therefore based on a system of representation that does not deny the original but aims rather to produce equivalence. To justify the bourgeoisie's production of the real, the system claims nature as the determinant referent. However, with the advent of the industrial revolution the metaphysical difference between being and appearance is abolished as the myth of equivalence achieves its apotheosis with the effacement of the original. With the technological revolution nature is no longer viewed as the determinant referent since it has in effect become the object of domination and exploitation. Although 'nature' during this phase of development still serves as a dissolved alibi, as the great referent, the Signified, it now only operates, 'under the objective stamp of Science, Technology and Production'.[5] Modernity is therefore to be distinguished from 'early modernity' in that it effects a substitution of the referent The (exploited) referent Nature is exchanged for the (exploiting) referent Man.

The transmutation of the referent also marks the transitional moment at which we move from an era of modernity to that of postmodernity. The third and final order of the simulacra occurs when the model or the code is elevated to the status of referent. It is an order which represents not an extension of capital in the Marxist sense that it is merely a continuation of the already progressively encroaching tide of capital, but a much more fundamental and structural mutation of every aspect of the functioning of the system. It is as it were the gravitational pull responsible for that tide. For now it is not capital but models that, 'precede all forms according to the modulation of their difference. Only affiliation with models makes sense, and nothing flows any longer according to its end, but precedes from the model, the 'signifier of reference', which is a kind of anterior finality and the only resemblance there is'.[6] The teleological principles that had sustained modernism's investiture in the referent man – Lyotard's narratives of progress and enlightenment – now collapse as the principles of space and time are telescoped into the operationality of the model. Taking for instance, the example of nuclear weapons, the 'Catch 22' of this formulation of postmodernism becomes strikingly apparent: We come 'out of history' shaking ourselves free of those teleological narratives that justified and apparently chained our future to the development of nuclear weapons, only to find that such liberation is utterly chimerical. The imperative to progress, with all the negative connotations that it held, disappears only when the system reaches maturity – when it becomes what Dick Hebdige, following Borges, terms 'Tlöns' – in other words self-referential, self-generating and recursive fictions. Paradoxically therefore, liberation from the nuclear threat only occurs after we have been irradiated and as a diversion from the real nuclearisation of our lives. This is an example of what might be termed the 'precession effect', whereby the model precedes and anticipates the logic of the event, thereby disarming and neutralising it.

As 'genetic codes and digitality' become the dominant operational principles of the postmodern era so everything becomes inserted into its definalised space–time and becomes disconnected from its own finalities as it is disintegrated and absorbed. The real is thus

> hyperrealised. Neither realised nor idealised: but hyperrealised. The hyperreal is the abolition of the real not by violent destruction, but by its assumption and elevation to the strength of the model. Anticipation, deterrence, preventative transfiguration etc ... the model acts as the sphere of absorption of the real.[7]

With the precession of the model everything becomes inserted into the depthless space of the simulacrum. Objects are now liberated from the substance of representation since they can no longer be conceived as mirroring the subject. The object now appears ingenious, impervious to the manipulations of the subject upon it. We are now implored to side with the dire or fatal object – the object that refuses to be spoken for, which refuses the garrulous discourse of meaning. Theory itself is now divided along similar lines, into what Baudrillard terms banal and fatal. The distinction is elucidated by Meaghan Morris: 'in the former, the subject believes itself always to be more malign than the object, while in the latter the object is always assumed to be more malign, more cynical, more brilliant than the subject ...'[8]

The banality of a theory or conviction that the space of the subject is in some way inviolable and sacrosanct is perhaps best illustrated with the example of the Loud family – the American family that submitted itself to seven months' uninterrupted filming in a TV *verite* experiment. The liturgical drama of the Loud family concluded in the spectacle of its disintegration. Whence, as Baudrillard points out, the insoluble controversy: Was TV responsible? What would have happened if TV had not been there?

> More interesting is the phantasm of filming the Louds *as if TV wasn't there*. The producer's trump card was to say: 'They lived as though we weren't there.' An absurd paradoxical formula – neither true nor false but utopian. The 'as if we weren't there' is equivalent to 'as if you weren't there'. It is this utopia, this paradox that fascinated 20 million viewers, much more than the perverse pleasure of prying. In this 'truth' experiment, it is neither a question of secrecy nor of perversion, but of a kind of thrill of the real, or of an aesthetics of the hyperreal, a thrill of vertiginous and phony exactitude, a thrill of alienation and magnification, of distortion in scale, of excessive transparency all at the same time. The joy in an excess of meaning, when the bar of the sign slips below the regular waterline of meaning: the non-signifier is elevated by the camera angle. Here the real can be seen to have never existed (but 'as if you were there'), without the distance that produces perspective space and our depth vision (but 'more true than nature'). Joy in the microscopic simulation that transforms the real into the hyperreal.[9]

In the case of the Loud family, the real has intermingled with the model to the extent that what is experienced is the loss of any transcendental space between subject and object, seeing and being seen, cause and effect. This is not just limited to the particular case of the Loud family, but a general condition; continual solicitation to play the media playing ourselves. We witness an implosive dissolution as life becomes TV and TV becomes life. In this reversed logic of social existence, the radiating model of causality and the differential model of determination intermingle freely as every position is absorbed by and absorbs its other, in a compulsive and imma-nent logic of reversal. What this signifies is a 'switching over from the panoptic apparatus of surveillance to a system of deterrence, where the distinction between active and passive is abolished'.[10] What is lost in the process of 'switching over' is the space of ideology excavated by repre-sentational distance and perspective. This shift is crucial to Baudrillard's articulation of postmodernity as a culture of the simulacrum. What is forfeited in such a move is faith in the very notion of ideology as either the basis of understanding, or the premise of critique. This is the real threat of the Baudrillardian text.

What Baudrillard is principally contesting, however, is not the notion of ideology *per se*, but rather the reference principle of the image, according to which it appears to refer to a real world, to real objects and to produce something that is anterior to it. In a passage in *Simulations*, he disrupts our day-to-day confidence in the realism of images and the solidity of their contract with the referent:

> Is any given bombing in Italy the work of leftist extremists, or of extreme right-wing provocation, or staged by centrists to bring every terrorist regime into disrepute and to shore up its own failing power, or again is it a police inspired scenario in order to appeal to public security? All of this is equally true, and the search for proof, indeed the objectivity of the fact does not check this vertigo of interpretation.[11]

Within this babel of media information, disinformation, suspicion and counter-suspicion, cause and effect freely intermingle. Every enunciation and every text is now plunged into crisis, as the perspectival coordinates that had functioned to locate the text within a determinate political/social space are dissolved and the images, codes, subjects and events flow and intersect independent of the referent. The result is the fascinating con-fusion of the story with the real event, the scandal with its media represen-tation. The moral outrage invoked by the 'acid house' phenomena occu-pies exactly this sort of precipitous space. Did it exist before being sanctioned and then renunciated by the tabloids? Did the headlines that focused on drug abuse act descriptively, as the result of *bona fide* investiga-tion, or did they in fact operate *prescriptively*, inclining an otherwise in-nocuous youth culture towards tabloid sensationalism – determining and coopting the course of events in advance? Events become fascinating precisely because the media model has preceded and anticipated the reality that it purports to describe. And this is exactly why such events no longer have meaning, 'not because they are insignificant in themselves, but because they have been preceded by models with which their own process can only coincide'.[12]

The black hole of the masses

We live, according to Baudrillard, in the shadow of the silent majorities, in a sort of baleful twilight at the intersection of the two constitutive forces of postmodernity: the media and the masses. Where once these two forces were thought to exist symbiotically, each benefiting from the dynamics of a dialectic – the one existing for the other: the media better to socialise and politicise the masses, and the masses to (re)present themselves accordingly, thereby guaranteeing the continuation of the dialectic – Baudrillard suggests that in our present era the poles of the dialectic have imploded and each has become immanent in the other. Neither can claim any 'reality' except perhaps as the collateral or alibi of their redetermination, since both have trouble with the referent. Neither can exist except in representation. The 'silent majority' is thus the imaginary referent of a sociological/ political imagination that can never exceed the representation of its codes (class, social status, race, sex, etc.) and therefore can never escape the tautological aporia that is both its subject and object. Against a 'sociological mass' Baudrillard says, 'The term "mass" is not a concept. It is a leitmotif of political demogoguey, a soft, sticky, lumpenanalytical notion ... The mass is without attribute, predicate, quality, reference. This is its definition, or [rather] lack of definition. It has no sociological reality.'[13]

But is it necessarily the case that because a term has no 'reference' or 'sociological reality', it has no meaning? Surprisingly, Baudrillard's own citation of the Borgesian allegory of simulation sheds light on the nature of such a loss of meaning. To use the Borgesian notion of the map/masses metaphorically, what Baudrillard seems to be claiming is that because the boundaries of a country are in a state of continual flux and revision the country therefore cannot exist. However, it was exactly the desire for an 'ideal coextensivity between the map and the territory' that constituted the madness of the cartographer's project. It is a 'mad project' because the territory exists only in the drawing of the map and thus coextensivity between the real and the representational territory can never be achieved: the difference between the map and the territory upon which the project depends is itself illusory. To claim, as Baudrillard does, that the term map/mass is meaningless, is then surely to reinvest in this madness, since it implies an era in which the territory could exceed the boundaries of its terms in some unspecified but none the less meaningful way.

However, the force of Baudrillard's argument rests on exactly this difference, since the masses and the media *now* exist as a single process, immanent to each other. Such immanence marks our entry into a period of postmodernity which must therefore reject the critical dogma that presents the media as the most subtle form of manipulative ideological apparatus. According to this account of the social, readers of the *Sunday Sport* and the *Face* can in fact no longer be distinguished from readers of the *Guardian* and *Ten 8* – both 'resist this imperative of rational communication ... they idolise the play of signs and stereotypes ... they reject the "dialectic" of meaning'.[14] The implication is that it now makes little difference whether the play of signs and stereotypes is constellated around issues of sexism, racism, fashion, politics or media analysis, since all possible subject positions have in effect been coopted and administered in advance by the model or the code. This is because 'Media, all media, information, all information act in two directions: outwardly they produce more of the social, inwardly they neutralise social relations and the social itself.'[15]

As polls, tests, referenda and the other devices of representation are pushed into the dimension of simulation, so the fugitive referent can now appear only as the subterfuge for the various models and operating principles that circulate within the simulating machine. The masses no longer express themselves, they are surveyed. They do not reflect upon themselves, but are tested. This does not mean that they do not exist but rather that their representation is no longer possible. As this space of representation implodes, so we move beyond the subject: 'it isn't a subject that does not speak, it is a silence that refuses to be spoken for in its name ... they can no longer be spoken for, articulated, represented ... no longer being [a] subject, they can no longer be alienated.'[16] There is a paradox here that infuses nearly all of Baudrillard's work. What he attempts to describe are exactly those areas of our culture that defy description, representation and reference – the masses whose silence refuses to be spoken for ... And yet Baudrillard's own discourse regarding this silence remains determinedly garrulous.

Plundering the language of astrophysics Baudrillard claims that 'the masses function as a gigantic black hole which inexorably inflects, bends and distorts all energy and light radiation approaching it: an implosive sphere in which the curvature of spaces accelerates, in which all dimensions curve back on themselves and "involve" to the point of annihilation, leaving in their stead only a sphere of potential engulfment.'[17] No longer capable either of representation or of reflecting an external world, the masses are presented as a site of infinite implosion into which all meaning is absorbed. Their response to the bombardment of stimuli, messages and tests is hyperconformity, neither resisting nor taking part in any (simulated) dialectic but passively absorbing it. In other words, they are cast as a vast and unresponsive couch potato, which with a brutal but cunning hyperlogic refuses to invest meaning in 'messages' or to elevate any imperative to the level of action. They simply demand more.

It is a logic which finds itself reflexed back into Baudrillard's own writing strategies. He, no less (and perhaps more) than the objectual mass that he (fails) to describe, cannot escape this implosive ambiance. In Mick Carter's words: 'The logic of the code (if not its control) presses with an equal insistence on all social categories, even those who imagine they have escaped its influence.'[18]

Attempting to describe that which has no reference leads to a prose style that has little similarity to the sober body of sociological critique: 'the social void is scattered with interstitial objects and crystalline clusters that spin around and coalesce in a cerebral chiaroscuro.'[19] Baudrillard invokes something that is at once generated and denied by the discourse that describes it. It is an example of what Meaghan Morris[20] terms the aggravation of the adjective outbidding its noun in an ecstasy of communication, the result of a refusal to resort to the primary oppositions of subject and object, critique and critiqued. Here, as Baudrillard appropriately points out, the correspondence is with the models of sub-atomic physics rather than representational sociology: 'the masses are simply an opaque blind stratum, like those clusters of stellar gas known only through analysis of their light spectrum.'[21] Neither of the entities that these discourses seek to describe exists, except as an unstable matrix of differential relations identified by the explanatory framework. As with the perversity of the postmodern relationship between image and reality, so with the social, it is once again the model that precedes and determines the 'reality' that it was designed and thought to describe.

Postmodernity, nihilism and death

Baudrillard describes a postmodernity predicated on death – the end of history, the social, meaning, politics, etc. – whilst offering no recipes or strategies of resistance, and refusing to posit alternatives. He is equally disrespectful to traditional Marxist notions of social revolution and to the molecular politics of resistance espoused by, for instance, Foucault, Deleuze and Guattari, since these are all still tied to the imperialist ideology of expansion. They are approaches that are 'explosive' – aiming to expand and redeploy collapsing subjectivity and failing political action across a wider social and cultural force field – and hence completely chimerical in a time of sustained implosion:

> To a system whose argument is oppression and repression, strategic resistance is the liberating claim of subjecthood. But this reflects rather the system's previous phase, and even if we are still confronted with it, it is no longer the strategic terrain: the system's current argument is the maximisation of the word and the maximal production of meaning. Thus the strategic resistance is that of a refusal of the word – or of the hyperconformist simulation of the very mechanism of the system, which is a form of refusal and non-reception.[22]

This is the refusal and non-reception we find in the silent majority whose inertia and silence refuses all dialectic and play of meaning. Against the acceleration of networks and circuits in the exchange of meaning the masses seek slowness and 'insurmountable immobility'. (We find a similar response enacted in the work of Andy Warhol who, in detailing the topography of contemporary metropolitan experience in terms of parody and hyperconformism, prefigures Baudrillard's mapping of everyday life in the 'Empire of Signs'.) In this ascent to extremes we too refuse the dialectic of oppositions and now must also combat the same with the same in a never-ending spiral of intensification: 'We will not seek change, nor oppose the fixed and the mobile; we will seek what is more mobile than mobile: metamorphosis . . . We will not distinguish the true from the false; we will seek what is more false than false: illusion and appearance . . .'[23] Although Baudrillard never elevates this strategy to the level of an imperative, the 'intensification of the same' now presents itself as the only response to a system whose strength lies in the capacity first to assimilate and then, ultimately, to simulate all forms of opposition.

Whereas in contemporary fascist or authoritarian regimes, the 'media' functions to provide the individual with the best possible reassurance that he/she lives in the best possible society, in so called 'liberal' democracies, a simulation of debate imposes the terms of what is to be discussed. A fiction is effectively created, by which the spectacle of conflicts between different social categories or political factions offers the satisfactory impression of real political liberty. Personal or communal salvation by means of revolutionary endeavour no longer seems desirable given the conviction that in all political projects lies the threat of tightening the social order. The fiction of liberty (and by implication 'real' oppositional possibilities) simply masks the silence of those who are not represented – who do not fit the system of representation – the silent majority.

To the principles of absorption and indifference are now opposed those of intensification and sameness. Baudrillard's writing can in this sense be seen as an attempt to force the present political system to reveal itself. He resists dialectic and even dialogue and instead challenges the system with a logic of provocation – since this is the only possible strategy when faced by a system whose main skill, as Jacques Daquerelle puts it, 'is one of recuperation and whose tolerance towards criticism hides its need for it – a need for participants all to agree to play the game, precisely the thing that Baudrillard's work refuses to do'.[24] The pleasure and the 'postmodernity' of the Baudrillardian text lies in this refusal to participate in existing ontologies. It is seductive rather than dialectic and challenges rather than communicates. It refuses to step outside – to impose the terms of the debate and assume a priority of the subject over the object. The text now becomes captor and captive, terrorist and hostage all at the same time. This is the sense in which it has achieved a curious sort of 'perfection' noted by Arthur Kroker: 'It is a "perfect text" because in its fragmentation of objects as particles in a vast semiurgy; in its refusal to participate in the fetishisation of the "real"; and its despair over awareness of *la manque* in experience, it is a transparent, but silently screaming, description of the "simulacrum" which is its *topos* of investigation.'[25]

Written into the 'perfection' of the Baudrillardian text is its own disappearance. In his recent work, critical distance has achieved a degree zero. From this point we are left with nothing but the seduction of a self-propagating negativity based on evacuation and dissolution. Negation and fatalism now collapse into one another leaving only an empty fascination with the very process of disappearance, indifference and neutralisation. It is a form of criticism that can no longer distance itself from its object, that now takes part in the pornographic abjection of the visible. Unable to confront anything, since it can achieve no distance from it, only the critical gesture remains – elusive and self-referential – perhaps nothing more than just a gross simulacrum of what it once was.

In both describing and partaking in the exhaustion of meaning that leads to a situation of undifferentiated equivalence, Baudrillard has become the exponent of a particularly postmodern nihilism of neutrality and indifference:

> Nihilism no longer has the dark, Wagnerian, Spenglerian complexion of the end of the century. It no longer arises from a *Weltanschauung* of decadence or from a metaphysical radicality born of the death of God and all the consequences that necessarily follow on from this. Nihilism today is a nihilism of transparency, and in a way it is more radical, more crucial than its earlier historical forms, for this transparency, this floating is irresolvably the floating of the system, and of all theory which claims to analyse it. When God is dead, Neitzsche was still there to say it – that great nihilist before the Eternal and the cadaver of the Eternal. But, before the simulated transparency of everything, before the simulacrum of the materialist or idealist completion of the world in hyperreality (God is not dead, he has become hyperreal), there is no longer any theoretical and critical God to recognise his own.[26]

Regarding Baudrillard as the spiritual heir of the condition that Neitzsche describes as that of the 'last man', the Australian critic Paul Foss points to the dereliction of Baudrillard's position by comparing this nihilism of transparency with that of its forefather. Where Nietzsche confronts negation and fatalism to evoke a sort of curvilinear re-experiencing or retesting of all challenges in a process of metamorphosis, Baudrillard offers no such procedure, accepting, instead, the collapse of value and eclipse of faith with an unresistant, glacial, moribund acceptance. Foss thus makes the useful distinction between the positive/active and the negative/ reactive nihilist. The former hopes for despair in order to be free for the possibility of hope. For him/her, value and significance, if they are to ground the real, restrict man's freedom with the chains of objectivity. Whereas the positive/active nihilist despairs of objectivity in order to be able to hope, the negative or reactive nihilist dissolves the chains of objectivity with the acid of despair only to resolve him/herself in the hope of hopelessness:

> The will becomes satisfied with meaninglessness, it finds comfort and even derives a certain happiness from the transparency assumed by a criticism deprived of the power of forging differences or explication: this 'obscene', all exteriorised form of criticism loses the teleological principle by which it could once challenge and repudiate reality: the weight of criticism dissipates into a kind of free falling objectivity doomed to meditate on its own errant course.[27]

This is, according to Foss, the course that Baudrillard has taken – a course that inflates the mundane and the platitudinous into significance and degrades the values and discriminations upon which critical discourse depends.

Past the post

Hostility towards postmodernism in general, and Baudrillard's more recent effusions in particular, has been guaranteed in part by the use of unfamiliar terminology and extended (non)descriptive passages that have little or nothing in common with the orthodox language of cultural criticism. Reaction to this later work has tended to fall into two camps. On the one hand there are those who seek 'use value' from *within* the text. Such a frustrated and frustrating reading tends to lead to a dismissal of this entire body of writing as merely partaking in a cult of deconstructive mysticism that, in renouncing criticism's traditional claims towards communication, interpretation, prescription, etc., can only lapse into a kind of doomed autism. On the other side we find a cult of devotees who exchange catchwords – fatal, viral, catastrophic, implosive, seductive – with the elaboracy of a Masonic ritual. Very little common ground can be found to be occupied between these two poles of reception and response: one is overtly hostile and antagonistic and the other celebratory, introverted and cabalistic. Paradoxically however, both concur in the characterisation of postmodernism as nebulous, tending towards a terminology that can only be described as labyrinthine. Indicating a degree of cultural consensus, at least regarding the issue of change (whether embraced or viewed with hostility), this must speak of a need to examine the specific vocabulary of postmodernism and its relationship to a culture in a state of transformation.

The excessive language to be found in the later Baudrillard can be seen as part of an attempt to avoid any pretensions to philosophical and political finality. A language and syntax is developed that can accommodate the sort of bizarre collisions and lateral or overlapping displacements that characterise the shifting surfaces of the postmodern problematic. Across this surface things are rarely stationary for long enough to indulge in narrative structures based on resolution or the revelation of source or origin. New rhetorical devices and enunciative strategies need to be evolved – strategies and devices that no longer presuppose a hierarchical ordering between subject and object, substance and shadow, reality and appearance. However, where the initial aim of these devices and strategies may have been to destructure a consciousness and rationality over-sure of itself and thus easy prey to subtle, and not so subtle, dogmatisms, they can now no longer presuppose the existence of the 'other' (of dogmatic rationalism) that they had set out to contest. Without this cultural 'other' against which destructuring intentions can be tested, we find that they are no longer directed outwards, but are now simply reflexed back into the text. It is a point made by Mick Carter, speaking specifically of Baudrillard, when he states that 'The purveyor of the notions of the death of meaning and the pervasiveness of simulacra has cut his cloth accordingly – implosion means not only the death of history, but also the blocking off of the possibility of writing about this death.'[28]

Postmodern death is doubly punitive – not only has the object died (or at least simulated its own death throes), but it has refused to die as a discrete entity. Death now spreads virally, taking with it not just the subject but also the subject's doomed articulations of his or her disappearance. This is symptomatically illustrated in Baudrillard's own ruminations upon the new viral aetiology of hyperrealism: 'It is in this promiscuity and ubiquity of images, in this viral contamination of things by images, that our obscenity exists.'[29] But we find exactly the same 'viral', contaminative processes operating within his own enunciations, as 'adjectives outbid nouns' in ecstatic rites of proliferation and intensification. The balance of opposites born of contradiction, difference and dialectic now becomes nothing more than semantic polarisation. Any one term can now be hyperbolically intensified until it becomes its opposite: 'Every characteristic thus elevated to the superlative power, caught in an intensifying spiral – more true than the true, more beautiful than the beautiful, more real than the real – is assured a vertiginous effect that is independent of all content and specific quality . . .'[30] It is also the effect of the Baudrillardian text which functions as both sign and symptom of the viral crisis that it announces.

The new viral and contaminative aetiology is no longer based on the dissected body of anatomical medicine but rather on Deleuze and Guattari's 'body without organs' – an inscribed surface of events, delocalised and merged with the 'schizz-flows' and networks of the non-space of simulation. The old medical terminology of surgical penetration, extraction, amputation, isolation and removal is no longer applicable to the postmodern body which refuses to 'anatomise', to become the sum of a number of discrete and isolated parts. The new rhetoric is founded on an entirely different metaphorical base. Now we learn to speak of immunisation, defence-systems and anti-bodies relating to different types of bodily contamination and devastation and specifically to perhaps the most 'postmodern' of illnesses, AIDS.

The language of cellular genetics has been expanded to become the language of postmodern culture generally.

The media, according to Baudrillard, has become like a genetic formula which controls the 'mutation of the real into the hyperreal'. It is a mutation which is viral and virulent. The real, which once existed as an organic interrelated whole, is now digitalised and particularised according to new codes and operational configurations. Events take on a capricious singularity as the atomic model of crisis in everyday life is exchanged for a viral model that only knows the effects of overcrowding and overprotection – contagion and the lack of any 'natural' immunity. Contamination, contiguity, proximity and promiscuity become the new lexicon of a structural breakdown that terrorises and ravages every aspect of the postmodern condition – the postmodern body subjected to AIDS, a postmodern culture in which stable meanings and grounding realities have been 'contaminated' by the instability and mutability of media simulations. Even postmodern nature, built according to Lyotard out of the data-banks which are the 'encyclopedias of tomorrow', is subject to viral affliction, as the computer program, like the body, becomes another site of contamination and contagion. Here we find individual and collective fates brought together under the paranoid umbrella which controls and polices the interaction, cross-fertilisation and emission of information as much as bodily fluids.

As speed and accessibility become the imperatives behind an information industry dependent on 'multi-user polylogue', so it has become an industry increasingly vulnerable to viral contamination. Transmitted through intercourse, interface and intention, the presence or suspected presence of the electronic virus generates the wholly new problem of electronic prophylaxis. At no time will this be more acute than with the introduction of fibre optic technology, which allows all media to intermingle on a single channel. As all media become standardised according to transmission frequency and bit format, overcrowding and contamination might threaten the exchange of any sort of 'uninfected' information. The irony is significant: the move towards fibre optics was initiated by a defence imperative based on the fact that nuclear explosions send high intensity electronic pulses through traditional copper cables, thus crippling the connected computer network at the moment of greatest need. The fact that the logic of information exchange presupposes an era of electronic warfare serves only to confirm the thesis put forward by Virilio in 'Pure War'[31] – that the threat of the *real* possibility, indeed the probability, of war during peacetime must be interpreted as a state of war in itself. The irony being that as the speed and sophistication of defence computing increases so the system as a whole becomes increasingly defenceless – as prone to the viral crisis within as resistant to the nuclear crisis without.

Along roughly similar lines Arthur Kroker outlines a correspondence between the medical rhetoric surrounding AIDS research and the military rhetoric of the Star Wars space defence programme. Both focus on the breakdown of immune systems:

> Both Star Wars and AIDS are theorised in the common research language of cellular genetics, where missiles are viruses and invading antigens body missiles. In both cases the strategic aim is for the immune system's B-cells (lasers in Star Wars; retroviruses in AIDS research) to surround invading antigens, whether within or without, in preparation for their destruction by cystoxic T-cells or killer cells.[32]

He goes on to point out that both deal with ruined surfaces, the body and the planet. He might well have added that both generate fear, in that they escape the traditional space of representation operating retroactively within an imploded temporal field.

The *panic* (both moral and otherwise) induced by the spectre of AIDS was also translated into the world of information electronics in the form of a computer virus crisis – graphically characterised in terms of something like AIDS stalking the tentacles of the world's electronic nervous system. The electronic virus, like its organic counterpart, escapes representation, operating parasitically, infiltrating and mutating existing programmes (or DNA commands). Minute variants of those routine programme structures allow the computer virus to operate exponentially without apparently affecting the form of the parent program or body. Typically a virus operates latently, with varying gestation periods, infiltrating its way through systems files and applications, simultaneously reproducing whilst covering its tracks. Corresponding remarkably closely to Baudrillard's account of the transmutation of the real into the hyper-real via the genetic code of the media – a code which is itself 'viral' – both appeal to a renewed sense of insecurity. As the computer virus threatens our sense of technological mastery, so the viral incursions of the media threaten the stability of our relationship to the 'outside' world. In each case it is an insecurity that takes on a particular intensity since the viral presence can be neither proved nor disproved until it is too late. Appearances are no longer trustworthy – the sign is no longer the symptom. And in Carter's words we are left with only 'a blasted hope that can no longer be certain of its premisses – in a simulated world everything is suspect, capable of seducing by its very ability to comfort the individual into believing that nothing has substantially changed and the world isn't lost.'[33]

Notes

1 Jean Baudrillard, *The Ecstasy of Communication* (Semiotext(e), 1988), p.22.
2 Baudrillard, 'The Evil Demon of Images' (Power Institute Publications, 1984) pp.25–6.
3 Baudrillard, *Simulations* (Semiotext(e), 1983), p.84.
4 Ibid., p.84.
5 Baudrillard, 'The Mirror of Production', trans. Mark Poster, *Telos*, 1975, p.54.
6 Baudrillard, *Simulations*, p.101.
7 Baudrillard, *In the Shadow of the Silent Majorities* (Semiotext(e), 1983) p.84.
8 Meaghan Morris, 'Room 101 Or A Few Worst Things In The World' in Andre Frankovits (ed.), *Seduced and Abandoned: The Baudrillard Scene* (Stonemoss, 1984) p.94.
9 Baudrillard, *Simulations*, p.50.
10 Ibid., p.53.
11 Ibid., p.31.
12 Baudrillard, 'The Evil Demon of Images', p.22.
13 Baudrillard, *In the Shadow of the Silent Majorities*, pp.4–5.
14 Ibid., p.10.
15 Ibid., p.66.
16 Ibid., p.22.
17 Ibid., p.9.
18 Mick Carter, 'From Red Centre to Black Hole' in Frankovits (ed.), *Seduced and Abandoned: The Baudrillard Scene*, p.74.
19 Baudrillard, *In the Shadow of the Silent Majorities*, p.3.
20 See Meaghan Morris, 'Room 101 Or A Few Worst Things In The World'.
21 Baudrillard, *In the Shadow of the Silent Majorities*, p.21.
22 Ibid., p.108.
23 Baudrillard, 'Fatal Strategies' in Mark Poster (ed.), *Jean Baudrillard: Selected Writings* Polity, 1988 p.185.
24 Jacques Daquerelle and John MacDonald, 'Resistance and Submission' in Frankovits (ed.), *Seduced and Abandoned: The Baudrillard Scene*, p.18.
25 Arthur Kroker and David Cook, *The Postmodern Scene: Excremental Culture and Hyper-Aesthetics* (St Martins Press, 1986) p.111.
26 Baudrillard, *Sur le Nihilism*, trans. Paul Foss (Galilee, 1981) p.229.
27 Paul Foss, 'Despero Ergo Sum' in Frankovits (ed.), *Seduced and Abandoned: The Baudrillard Scene*, p.27.
28 Carter, 'From Red Centre to Black Hole' in Frankovits (ed.), *Seduced and Abandoned: The Baudrillard Scene*, pp.73–4.
29 Baudrillard, *The Ecstasy of Communication*, pp.35–6.

30 Baudrillard, 'Fatal Strategies' in Mark Poster (ed.), *Jean Baudrillard: Selected Writings*, p.186.
31 See Paul Virilio, *Pure War* (Semiotext(e) 1983).
32 Arthur and Marilouise Kroker, *Body Invaders: Sexuality and the Postmodern Condition* (Macmillan, 1988) pp.12–13.
33 Carter, 'From Red Centre to Black Hole' in Frankovits (ed.), *Seduced and Abandoned: The Baudrillard Scene*, p.76.

Postscript

Surveying postmodernity from the precipice of the 'end', Baudrillard describes a culture which is not just prone to, but actually predicated on, instability and uncertainty. Everything has become short-circuited within the whirligig of reflexivity and paradox. Sober analysis has been displaced by 'virulent description' (more descriptive than description: hype[1]). Linear argument is turned back upon itself, looping around into a closed circuit. This circular logic is a feature not just of Baudrillard's own work but is also reflexed into the writing strategies of his critics and commentators – this one no less than any other. To a certain extent this book reproduces the progressive exhaustion of meaning that it seeks to trace and analyse. As with Baudrillard's own work, the writing style becomes labyrinthine and nebulous as the theoretical ground upon which we are forced to tread becomes increasingly paradoxical and treacherous. How, after all, do we meaningfully enunciate the end of meaning? How do we *critique* a text which is premissed on a denial of the possibility of meaning, let alone of critique? Can we really describe how things really are not (in other words the loss of reality)? Here the reflexive play of language confounds every attempt at analysis. The imperative to develop ever more fantastic formulae for contemporary crisis is only understandable in the context of this greater crisis of articulation. The old language is forcibly discarded, since it remains tied to the older order of things – to an era which presumed and even presupposed the presence or existence of incontrovertible facts, objective truths, the space of dialectic and the perspective of linear time (history). The language of postmodernism, though often overblown, is much less presumptuous. In renouncing critical distance and representational perspective, the old Euclidean geometry of critique (with subjects/objects, insides/outsides firmly differentiated), it suggests the emergence of a new theoretical curvature: 'Things aspire to be straight, like light in an orthoganal space, but they all have a secret curvature. Seduction is that which follows this curvature, subtly accentuating it until things, in following their own cycle, reach the superficial abyss where they are dissolved.'[2] Dialectical critique mistakes this secret curvature for the 'straightness' that it simulates. In seeking truth within the apparently linear configuration of theory, dialectical reason misses the point that things (even metaphysical things) are already bent, refracted and contorted. The

149

critic is secretly disarmed. Seeing the 'truth' requires us to discard exactly those critical procedures that allowed us to discern it, and to verify it for what it is. Every point along this 'secret curvature' is now an inversion not just of what has gone before, but also of the consciousness it has or had of itself. And instead of the old perspectives we are left with a series of obscene close-ups of nothing in particular ('At times ... Baudrillard is like a persistent neighbour who insists on showing you his out-of-focus holiday snaps[3]).

Along this curvature we are also committed to a state of perpetual (ecstatic) catastrophe – the fatality of Baudrillard's 'fatal strategies'. Meaghan Morris provides the most articulate account of the fatality of this shortcircuiting of history and the present, apeing Baudrillard and claiming that:

> The human species has passed the dead point of history: we are living out the ecstasy of permanent catastrophe, which slows down as it becomes more and more intense (une catastrophe au relenti, slow motion or slowing motion catastrophe), until the supereventfulness of the event approaches the uneventfulness of absolute inertia, and we begin to live everyday catastrophe as an endless dead point, or a perpetual freeze frame.[4]

To escape the numbing, stupefying fascination of catastrophic theory perhaps we should attempt to recover what Canetti originally termed the 'dead point' in history, to 'locate this blind spot beyond which "things have ceased to be real", where history has ceased to exist, without us realising it, and where, lacking such insight, we can only persevere in our current destruction?'[5] In other words, we are being asked to search amnesiacally for the point at which we lost our cultural memory. Baudrillard regards it as pious and moralistic to attempt to search for such a point as if it were the moment at which we made some error or committed some fatal imprudence. But here he misses the point, mistaking a way of being (or theorising) for a finalised state (or teleology). We may well be living in a state of 'perpetual catastrophe' but the fatality that such a state implies rests on the difference, as George Alexander puts it, between wish (with its implied resignation) and will. He recounts this vision of catastrophe in terms of the daily drama of getting up in the morning:

> You are lying in bed on a cold morning paralysed between two extremes: the warmth of the bed and the cruel cold of the room. You toss between warm/cold, warm/cold, yes/no, yes/no ... and tell yourself, this is terrible, I must get up. You are paralysed because the idea of rising is kept in the condition of wish, not will. And then at some catastrophic point – without struggle or decision, you find suddenly that you've arisen.[6]

A similar state of suspended paralysis affects (infects) Baudrillard's account of postmodern subjectivity. Here too we find a stultifying fascination with the disappearance of will, the disappearance of the self in the commutability of its terms – warm/cold, yes/no, self/other. Like the person lying in bed who fails to reach Alexander's 'catastrophic point', Baudrillard's postmodern subject never escapes from the shade of his/her own formula. He/she remains blank, decentred, a pure receiving screen existing in the passive state of wish without will. Like the TV screen it is a subjectivity that flickers between alternatives, never settling, never finding a narrative closure. Employing schizophrenia and schizoid ontology as the model/metaphor of this 'fatal' state, Baudrillard insists on 'implosion' as opposed to 'drift', 'collapse' rather than 'deconstruction', 'dispersal' rather than 'deterritorialisation'. The self become TV. But there are many ways of watching TV, and not all of them desensitised and undemanding – even given a personal predilection for the latter. TV does not always traverse us as if across the exposed terminals of Baudrillard's 'pure receiving screen' despite the flow of TV being in many ways the flow of postmodern life. But instead of resignation (the Baudrillardian effect of disappearance) we must, as Deleuze and Guatarri suggest, cut and intersect the flow of simulation, to effect a *decoupage* and find new (vital) lines of escape. In other words not to attempt to step outside the flow, but to reterritorialise the self within it, to ambush it as we assimilate it.

Effort must now be shifted away from the nostalgic project of reappropriating a lost 'being' that existed prior to the fatality of simulation. Fatal strategies must be replaced with vital strategies and the state of wish must now become that of will.

We might finally reflect on the narrative closure of this postscript – this end as both sign and symptom of the many 'ends' that the text has announced. Conclusions traditionally serve to escort the reader home. But there are no homes. As one critic put it: 'Hyperreality is a nice place to visit, but you wouldn't want to live there.'[7] So all that we are left with is a nostalgia for an era that existed prior to simulation, for a stability that we cannot find in the text. We may hope for a conclusion – for something like the traditional retrospective summary-and-judgement – a stentorian voice to restore balance and perspective to an otherwise imbalanced and volatile world. But such a return to the sanctuary of the critical voice is precisely what is denied by the trajectory of postmodern discourse. Instead we find ourselves left with something much more modest, but perhaps more urgent. That is the task, not of finding ends, solutions and finalities, but of living in a world from which these privileges and certainties have been withdrawn.

Notes

1 See Meaghan Morris, 'Room 101 Or A Few Worst Things In The World' in Frankovits (ed.) *Seduced and Abandoned* (Stonemoss, 1984).

2 Jean Baudrillard, *The Ecstasy of Communication* (Semiotext(e), 1987), p.70.
3 See 'Baudrillard's About' in the *Face*.
4 Morris, 'Banality in Cultural Studies', *Block*, 14, 1988, p.19.
5 Baudrillard, 'Fatal Strategies' in Poster (ed.), *Jean Baudrillard: Selected Writing* (Polity, 1988), p.191.
6 George Alexander, 'Les Maitres Fou, The Signifying Monkey on the Planet of the Postmodern', *Futurefall: Excursions into Post-Modernity* (Power Institute Publications, 1986) pp.45–6.
7 Ibid., p.43.